MISSION 85

The Stackpole Military History Series

THE AMERICAN CIVIL WAR
Cavalry Raids of the Civil War
Ghost, Thunderbolt, and Wizard
In the Lion's Mouth
Pickett's Charge
Witness to Gettysburg

WORLD WAR I
Doughboy War

WORLD WAR II
After D-Day
Airborne Combat
Armor Battles of the Waffen-SS,
    1943–45
Armoured Guardsmen
Army of the West
Arnhem 1944
Australian Commandos
The B-24 in China
Backwater War
The Battle of France
The Battle of Sicily
Battle of the Bulge, Vol. 1
Battle of the Bulge, Vol. 2
Beyond the Beachhead
Beyond Stalingrad
The Black Bull
Blitzkrieg Unleashed
Blossoming Silk against the Rising Sun
Bodenplatte
The Brandenburger Commandos
The Brigade
Bringing the Thunder
The Canadian Army and the Normandy
    Campaign
Coast Watching in World War II
Colossal Cracks
Condor
A Dangerous Assignment
D-Day Bombers
D-Day Deception
D-Day to Berlin
Decision in the Ukraine
Destination Normandy
Dive Bomber!
A Drop Too Many
Eagles of the Third Reich
The Early Battles of Eighth Army
Eastern Front Combat
Europe in Flames
Exit Rommel
The Face of Courage
Fist from the Sky
Flying American Combat Aircraft of
    World War II
For Europe
Forging the Thunderbolt
For the Homeland
Fortress France

The German Defeat in the East,
    1944–45
German Order of Battle, Vol. 1
German Order of Battle, Vol. 2
German Order of Battle, Vol. 3
The Germans in Normandy
Germany's Panzer Arm in World War II
GI Ingenuity
Goodwood
The Great Ships
Grenadiers
Guns against the Reich
Hitler's Nemesis
Hold the Westwall
Infantry Aces
In the Fire of the Eastern Front
Iron Arm
Iron Knights
Japanese Army Fighter Aces
Japanese Naval Fighter Aces
JG 26 Luftwaffe Fighter Wing War Diary,
    Vol. 1
JG 26 Luftwaffe Fighter Wing War Diary,
    Vol. 2
Kampfgruppe Peiper at the Battle of
    the Bulge
The Key to the Bulge
Knight's Cross Panzers
Kursk
Luftwaffe Aces
Luftwaffe Fighter Ace
Luftwaffe Fighter-Bombers over Britain
Luftwaffe Fighters and Bombers
Massacre at Tobruk
Mechanized Juggernaut or Military
    Anachronism?
Messerschmitts over Sicily
Michael Wittmann, Vol. 1
Michael Wittmann, Vol. 2
Mission 85
Mission 376
Mountain Warriors
The Nazi Rocketeers
Night Flyer / Mosquito Pathfinder
No Holding Back
On the Canal
Operation Mercury
Packs On!
Panzer Aces
Panzer Aces II
Panzer Aces III
Panzer Commanders of the
    Western Front
Panzergrenadier Aces
Panzer Gunner
The Panzer Legions
Panzers in Normandy
Panzers in Winter
Panzer Wedge, Vol. 1
Panzer Wedge, Vol. 2

The Path to Blitzkrieg
Penalty Strike
Poland Betrayed
Red Road from Stalingrad
Red Star under the Baltic
Retreat to the Reich
Rommel's Desert Commanders
Rommel's Desert War
Rommel's Lieutenants
The Savage Sky
Ship-Busters
The Siege of Küstrin
The Siegfried Line
A Soldier in the Cockpit
Soviet Blitzkrieg
Stalin's Keys to Victory
Surviving Bataan and Beyond
T-34 in Action
Tank Tactics
Tigers in the Mud
Triumphant Fox
The 12th SS, Vol. 1
The 12th SS, Vol. 2
Twilight of the Gods
Typhoon Attack
The War against Rommel's Supply Lines
War in the Aegean
War of the White Death
Winter Storm
Wolfpack Warriors
Zhukov at the Oder

THE COLD WAR / VIETNAM
Cyclops in the Jungle
Expendable Warriors
Fighting in Vietnam
Flying American Combat Aircraft:
    The Cold War
Here There Are Tigers
Land with No Sun
MiGs over North Vietnam
Phantom Reflections
Street without Joy
Through the Valley
Two One Pony

**WARS OF AFRICA AND THE
MIDDLE EAST**
Never-Ending Conflict
The Rhodesian War

GENERAL MILITARY HISTORY
Carriers in Combat
Cavalry from Hoof to Track
Desert Battles
Doughboy War
Guerrilla Warfare
Ranger Dawn
Sieges
The Spartan Army

MISSION 85

The U.S. Eighth Air Force's Battle over Holland, August 19, 1943

Ivo de Jong

STACKPOLE
BOOKS

Published in the United States in 2013 by
STACKPOLE BOOKS
5067 Ritter Road
Mechanicsburg, PA 17055
www.stackpolebooks.com

Cover design by Tracy Patterson

Printed in the United States of America

10 9 8 7 6 5 4 3 2 1

Library of Congress Cataloging-in-Publication Data

Jong, Ivo de, 1963–
    Mission 85 : the U.S. Eighth Air Force's battle over Holland, August 19, 1943 /
Ivo de Jong.
        pages cm. — (Stackpole military history series)
    "Originally published in the Netherlands by Liberation Museum 1944 in 1996."
    Includes index.
    ISBN 978-0-8117-1201-9
    1. United States. Air Force. Air Force, 8th—History—20th century.   2. World
War, 1939–1945—Campaigns—Netherlands.   3. World War, 1939–1945—Aerial
operations, American.   4. Bombing, Aerial—Netherlands.   5. Netherlands—
History—German occupation, 1940–1945.   I. Title.   II. Title: U.S. Eighth Air
Force's battle over Holland, August 19, 1943.   III. Title: Mission eighty five.
IV. Title: Mission eight five.
    D790.228th .J65 2013
    940.54'2192—dc23
                                                                      2012045018

It is usually presumed that combat flying is a fast, dangerous life, and I suppose that such is the case. It is remarkable, however, how immune one becomes to danger and to death from performances of duty. None of us, I am sure, minimized in his mind the hazards of flak and fighter planes. None of us were complete fatalists, able to dismiss the possibility of injury or death on any flight. And yet such a life becomes as prosaic and commonplace as any other. The "grim reaper" beckoned to each of us and hovered constantly among us, chasing here and there and selecting from time to time crews and individuals for his own. Strangely enough, his choices always surprised us, and many good men were marked and taken with whom one had been conversing a few hours previous and whom one fully expected to see at mess or the club that evening. For all that, we became anesthetized to the idea of dying or to harm. Death or injury was a possibility or a fact to us. Such things became not tragedies, but events, and we did not emotionalize the obvious.

—Dwight M. Curo, navigator, 303rd Bomb Group

For the boys

Dear God, you summoned them to serve
    Your Air Force far away;
Although we'd rather have them here,
    It's not for us to say.
We know the Spirit carries on
    when bones return to clay.
We feel that flesh of man may waste
    and soul still not decay.
We question not your reasoning
    in calling them away.
And only ask of you to grant
    this prayer for them today.
That they may find a happy home
    out there where blue meets grey.
    AMEN

—Russell G. Chester, radio operator,
381st Bomb Group

Contents

Foreword

The U.S. Eighth Air Force was activated in Savannah, Georgia, on January 28, 1942, and I had the pleasure of being assigned to the initial Bomber Command cadre. General Ira Eaker arrived in England in February 1942 and began the process building a staff who planned and obtained airfields and other facilities required for the initial combat units. In December 1942, General Eaker, now commander of the Eighth Air Force, traveled to Casablanca and was successful in convincing heads of state and top military leaders that combined round-the-clock British night and American daylight attacks against German targets were the best use of air power.

The initial Eighth Air Force bombing attack of August 17, 1942, was followed by a period of trying out new equipment and gaining battle experience. Most of the 1942 and 1943 missions were to relatively short-range targets in France and the Netherlands, with a few missions to German cities, such as Wilhelmshaven, Bremen, and Hamburg. These early missions developed the bombing techniques and leaders required for the late 1943 and the 1944 and 1945 massive missions.

In early August 1943, I was honored to become the commanding officer of the 303rd Bombardment Group (Heavy), the "Hell's Angels." I led my group on the first-anniversary mission of the Eighth Air Force, to Schweinfurt. Although overall losses were severe that day, the 303rd Bombardment Group lost no bombers.

Just two days later, the hard lesson that missions should not be labeled "milk runs" until after safe return from them was brought home to us. Two of our ships failed to return from Gilze-Rijen. One was actually the very same aircraft in which I had flown to Schweinfurt, with many men of my Schweinfurt lead crew aboard.

War was a deadly business, both for us in the air and for the people on the ground. Although we always tried our utmost to obtain pinpoint accuracy, it was inevitable that our bombs missed sometimes. However, as the war progressed, the Germans became acutely aware that the Eighth Air Force had earned its postwar name of "Mighty Eighth," as their ability to wage war declined as a result of our bombing effectiveness. The proud 303rd

Bombardment Group was one of the pioneer groups and played a vital role throughout the American air war in Europe.

It is good that one of the smaller missions to obtain our final goal, the destruction of Nazism, has been described in detail. I hope that future generations will never forget the sacrifices that were made for their freedom.

Colonel Kermit D. Stevens, USAF (Ret.)
Commanding Officer, 303rd Bombardment Group (H),
August 5, 1943, to September 1, 1944

Preface

With the attacks on the ball-bearing factory in Schweinfurt and the Messerschmitt aircraft factory in Regensburg on August 17, 1943, the U.S. Eighth Army Air Force marked the anniversary of its very first combat mission in the European theater of operations. Losses on this anniversary day were severe; no fewer than sixty bombers and their crews failed to return to their bases. It has become probably the best known of nearly a thousand missions that the Eighth Air Force flew during the war and thus became the subject of several books and documentaries.

Two days later, on August 19, the Eighth went on the warpath again—this time not to targets deep in Germany, but on a shallow penetration to airfields in southwestern Holland and Belgium. But the German *Luftwaffe* again rose to the challenge and furious aerial battles ensued over Holland. In contrast to Schweinfurt and Regensburg, this mission is now barely a footnote in the history of the airwar over Europe, and up to now, not one single book has been written about it.

In this book, an effort is made to describe and analyze the events of August 19, 1943. First, some insight will be given into the build-up of the Eighth Air Force and the way it conducted operations in this phase of the war. Then attention will be paid to attacks by medium bombers and fighters over northern France before the main attacks. These, the B-17 attacks on the Flushing, Gilze-Rijen, and Woensdrecht airfields, will be covered in more detail, forming the main topic of the book.

I have used many official reports (American, British, German, and Dutch) to get a historically accurate "framework." However, to make this account really come to life, I decided to use as much oral history as possible. These stories, coming from diaries, letters, or memory, were obtained through intensive correspondence with dozens of veterans and eyewitnesses. Their help was indispensable during my research and is gratefully acknowledged.

I hope that this book will give the readers insight into "just a day's work," an ordinary mission, of the Eighth Air Force and its consequences. Some of these consequences are still painfully felt today, by the families of those who died that day as a result of Mission 85, a milk run that turned sour.

CHAPTER 1

Setting the Scene

After the United States had entered the war in December 1941, immediate steps were taken to augment the bombing offensive on Germany. Until that time, this was carried out only by the British Royal Air Force, operating mainly at night. A small group of American staff officers, commanded by Brig. Gen. Ira C. Eaker, flew over to England, set up a headquarters, close to that of Royal Air Force Bomber Command, at High Wycombe, and started the build-up of the U.S. Eighth Army Air Force. In the first half of 1942, the first bombardment groups arrived in England, and after a few attacks by medium bombers, the first attack by heavy bombers—a mere twelve B-17s— was made on the Rouen marshalling yards on August 17, 1942.

Although the Royal Air Force had found out early in the war that bombing raids during the daylight hours resulted in unsustainable heavy losses, the American staff officers stuck to the daylight precision-bombing concept. With the armament on their force's heavy bombers, the B-17 Flying Fortress and B-24 Liberator, they believed they could battle their way to and from any target and bomb it accurately with the precision bombsight manufactured by Norden. This theory was put to the test, starting on this August 17, 1942, over Rouen.

The year that followed, which ended with the raids on Schweinfurt and Regensburg, can be divided into three phases. The first was the phase in which only shallow penetrations in the occupied countries were made. Main targets then were submarine pens in France and airfields close to the coastline. Most of these missions were flown with fighter escort available to the raiders. Losses to flak and enemy fighters were acceptable to American standards.

The second phase started with the attack on Wilhelmshaven on January 27, 1943. This was the first American attack on a target in Germany itself, and the Eighth Air Force now gradually expanded the range of its operations. This was not only because of the fact that the staff of the Eighth Air Force felt they were already strong enough to do so, but more because of the fact that the concept of the daylight bombing of Germany had to be proven in order to get more planes and replacement crews.

1

If the Eighth Air Force wasn't getting any more results beyond just attacking targets in the occupied countries, the much-needed replacements, coming from the United States, might be sent to another theater of operations, such as the Pacific or North Africa. It was to this last theater that the two oldest bomb groups of the Eighth Air Force, the 97th and 301st, had already been transferred in November 1942, much to the dismay of General Eaker.

In the first half of 1943, more and more attacks on Germany itself were mounted, besides the still ongoing attacks on targets in the occupied countries. However, the targets in Germany were mainly on the fringe of its territory, in cities such as Kiel, Bremen, Hamburg, Cuxhaven, and Emden. The majority of these missions in this phase was executed without fighter escort.

In May 1943, the Allied Combined Chiefs of Staff, approved of the so-called Pointblank Directive. In this directive, the targets were selected whose destruction would paralyze Germany's war effort and economy. Six target systems were proposed, comprising seventy-six precision targets to be destroyed by heavy bombers. They were to be directed against the three major elements of the German military machine, the submarine fleet, air force and ground force, and certain industries vital to their support. These six systems were

- Submarine construction yards and bases
- Aircraft industry
- Ball bearings
- Oil
- Synthetic rubber and tires
- Military transport vehicles

Besides listing these target systems and discussing their priority, the chief of staff clearly recognized certain intermediate objectives: "The Germans, recognizing the vulnerability of their vital industries, are rapidly increasing the strength of their fighter defenses. The German fighter strength in Western Europe is being augmented. If the growth of this German fighter strength is not arrested quickly, it may become literally impossible to carry out the destruction planned and thus create the conditions necessary for ultimate decisive action by our combined forces on the continent."

The third phase saw frequent attacks on airfields, aircraft factories, and repair facilities as a direct consequence of this statement. But the precision bombing of the German industry went on.

On June 22, the Eighth Air Force attacked a target deep in Germany for the first time. The target was a synthetic rubber plant in Huls in the Ruhr industrial area. The bombing results were encouraging and losses not excessive.

The aircrew are boarding B-17F 42-5763 *Bomb-Boogie* of the 91st Bomb Group for a combat mission. Walking on the right is 1st Lt. Elwood D. Arp, who flew *Bomb-Boogie* to Gilze-Rijen on August 19. CHAUNCEY H. HICKS

At the end of July 1943, the total combat strength of the Eighth Air Force had grown to nineteen heavy bomb groups, of which sixteen were equipped with the B-17, organized into the First and Fourth Bombardment Wings. The remaining three were equipped with the B-24 and constituted the Second Bombardment Wing.

These bomb groups, their airfields in England, and the dates of their first operational missions follow:

First Bombardment Wing

91 BG	Bassingbourn	November 7, 1942
92 BG	Alconbury	September 6, 1942
303 BG	Molesworth	November 17, 1942
305 BG	Chelveston	November 17, 1942
306 BG	Thurleigh	October 9, 1943
351 BG	Polebrook	May 14, 1943
379 BG	Kimbolton	May 29, 1943
381 BG	Ridgewell	June 22, 1943
384 BG	Grafton Underwood	June 22, 1943

Second Bombardment Wing

44 BG	Shipdham	November 7, 1942
93 BG	Hardwick	October 9, 1942
389 BG	Hethel	July 9, 1943

Fourth Bombardment Wing

94 BG	Bury St Edmunds	May 13, 1943
95 BG	Horham	May 13, 1943
96 BG	Snetterton Heath	May 14, 1943
100 BG	Thorpe Abbotts	June 25, 1943
385 BG	Great Ashfield	July 17, 1943
388 BG	Knettishall	July 17, 1943
390 BG	Framlingham	August 12, 1943

The formations flown in combat by the American bombers were subject to much study and consequent adaptions during the war. The purpose was to have the bombers provide maximum mutual covering defensive fire, to obtain a concentrated bombing strike, and, at the same time, to keep the formation manageable. Therefore, the basic building block for a bomber formation was a squadron, normally six B-17s flying in two elements of three aircraft. Sometimes, one or two B-17s filled in the so-called "diamond position" in the rear of such a squadron.

Three of these squadrons, called lead, high, and low and flying in this respect to each other, made up a group formation. This would thus comprise eighteen to twenty B-17s. A bomb group would normally put up a single group formation from its assignment of aircraft and aircrew. However, combat losses, personnel shortages, or mechanical troubles sometimes caused bomb groups to drop below the required number. Then two, or even three, bomb groups put up one or two squadrons each, which would then make a so-called composite group. On August 19, 1943, several of these composite groups would be in the sky over Holland and Belgium.

Within each group formation, the very first ship carried the mission leader, flying with the lead crew, which was usually very experienced and well on its way to finishing its tour of operations of twenty-five combat missions.

Three group formations, again called lead, high, and low, then made up a combat wing. It thus counted from fifty-four to sixty B-17s. Of course, each wing had its own wing lead crew, thus flying in the first ship of the lead squadron of the lead group.

In late June 1943, all three Liberator-equipped bomb groups of the Second Bombardment Wing were temporarily detached to North Africa. They were to execute a low-level attack on the oil refineries near Ploesti, Romania, together with bomb groups of the Ninth Air Force, which were already stationed in North Africa. After flying several smaller missions, the daring attack on Ploesti took place on August 1. Although it resulted in heavy damage to the refineries, it also brought severe losses for the raiders. No fewer than 52 of the 179 dispatched Liberators were shot down. The bomb groups

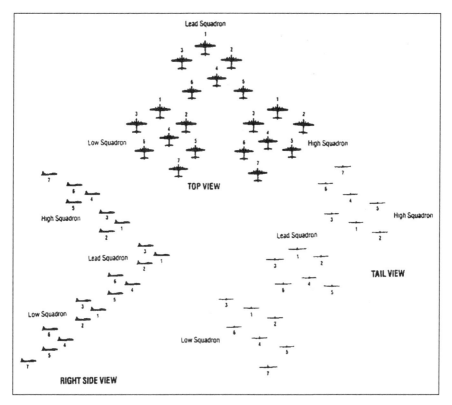

Eighth Air Force B-17 bomb groups flew this standard combat formation of twenty aircraft in August 1943 as part of the larger sixty-ship combat wing. The group formation was 380 meters wide, 210 meters deep, and 300 meters high. The formation positions of the vulnerable number 7 "diamond" or "tail-end-Charlie" ships varied widely. If the tail view of the group shown in the diagram is considered the lead group, the high group would trail it above and to the left, and the low group would trail below and to the right. JOHN WATERS INC. VIA BRIAN D. O'NEILL

of the Second Bombardment Wing did not return to England until late August and therefore played no part in the August 19 mission over Holland.

Meanwhile, the B-17 bomb groups of the First and Fourth Bombardment Wings had undertaken the most complicated and dangerous mission in the Eighth Air Force's history so far, on the anniversary of its first mission, August 17.

The nine bomb groups in the First Bombardment Wing had attacked the ball-bearing factory in Schweinfurt and suffered the loss of 36 of the 230 dispatched bombers. Where some units returned to England virtually unscathed, others were badly mauled. The 381st Bomb Group, for example, lost eleven of its ships with their crews; the 91st Bomb Group lost ten. It is obvious that no combat unit can sustain losses like these without suffering a drop in crew moral and combat readiness.

The seven bomb groups in the Fourth Bombardment Wing had attacked the Messerschmitt aircraft factory in Regensburg and lost 24 of their 146 bombers. Here again, some bomb groups bore the brunt of the German fighter attacks. The 100th Bomb Group lost ten ships; the 390th Bomb Group, on only its third combat mission, lost six.

The main feature of this attack on Regensburg was that the participating bombers did not return to England after dropping their load over the target. They continued on course, flying south over the Alps, over the Mediterranean, and finally landed on fields in North Africa. The majority of these bombers and their crews did not return to their English bases before August 24, when they bombed the Bordeaux/Merignac airfield on the way back. These crews also couldn't participate in the August 19 mission.

Besides the sixty bombers that were lost on the mission, eleven B-17s were damaged beyond economical repair, and many more required minor or major repairs by their ground crews.

In the summer of 1943, the Eighth Air Force also counted four bomb groups equipped with the B-26 Marauder medium bomber. Later that year, these units would be assigned to the Ninth Air Force. These groups, their bases, and dates of first operational mission were

322 BG	Andrews Field	May 14, 1943
323 BG	Earls Colne	July 16, 1943
386 BG	Boxted	July 30, 1943
387 BG	Chipping Ongar	August 15, 1943

The Marauder had a bad start in the European theater. After the first mission for the 322nd Bomb Group, a low-level attack on a power station on the Dutch coast, failed to bring about the destruction of the target, it was decided to repeat the attack three days later. On May 17, all ten Marauders that entered Dutch airspace were shot down by flak and fighters. No more low-level attacks were executed after this tragedy. From that day on, the Marauders were mainly used for bombing missions from medium altitude on targets near the Dutch, Belgian, and French coasts. These missions were often used as diversionary attacks for those of the heavy bombers. If these, for example, were to attack Germany and cross Holland on their route in, the Marauders would bomb airfields in northern France or Belgium some hours in advance. On August 19, 1943, three of these bomb groups would be in action over northern France.

P-47C 41-6330 of the 56th Fighter Group. On August 19, it was flown by Col. Hubert A. Zemke. It then carried the fuselage code LM-Z. These fuselage codes greatly improved visual identification of Allied aircraft. Two letters identified the squadron (for example, LM for the 62nd Fighter Squadron, UN for the 63rd Fighter Squadron). The single letter was the individual aircraft letter. usaaf

The "little friends" of the bomber crews, the fighter pilots, still had to turn back from escort duty when they approached the German border due to the limited fuel capacity of their planes. In August 1943, the Eighth Air Force Fighter Command consisted of only four operational fighter groups, all equipped with the sturdy P-47 Thunderbolt:

4 FG	Debden	October 2, 1942
56 FG	Halesworth	April 13, 1943
78 FG	Duxford	April 13, 1943
353 FG	Metfield	August 12, 1943

Fighter Command used the fighter group as its basic tactical unit. Just like the bomb group, the fighter group usually had its own airfield and was commanded by a colonel. But whereas the bomb group had four squadrons, the fighter group had only three. But these consisted of more planes, around thirty per squadron. The normal strength that a fighter group put up on a mission was forty-eight fighters, all three squadrons providing four flights of four planes each. A flight was then further divided into two sections of two planes each.

Every fighter squadron had its own radio call sign and the flights within it were referred to as white, red, blue, and green, respectively. Within the flight, number 1 was the leader, covered by his wingman, number 2; in turn, number 3 was covered by number 4. Thus, by using short call signs, everyone was directly able to identify the one who had sent a radio message. (For example, "Postgate Red 4" was the pilot in the number 4 position of the red flight in the 63rd Fighter Group.) This was quite essential when, during air battles, fractions of a second could mean the difference between life and death for a fighter pilot.

Fighter escort for the bombers was also regularly provided by the British Royal Air Force, which often put its Spitfire squadrons at the Eighth Air Force's disposal. After the *Luftwaffe*'s daylight threat over England had virtually disappeared, the Royal Air Force still kept many squadrons and their Spitfires in England, despite desperate pleas by commanders in other operational theaters. Generally, the Spitfire pilots in England were only too glad to be able to get in a fight with the *Luftwaffe* over continental Europe. Within the Royal Air Force, there were quite a few squadrons manned by non-Commonwealth pilots: Poles, Czechs, Norwegians, Frenchmen, Belgians, or Dutchmen. Many of these would see action on August 19, as we will see.

CHAPTER 2

The Plan

The operations by the Allied air forces on August 19 would commence with several fighter sweeps by RAF Typhoons over northern France and attacks by medium bombers of USAAF and RAF on airfields in that same area.

Three sweeps by Typhoons were scheduled. They were to provoke a reaction by the *Luftwaffe* and help divert its attention from the attacks by the more vulnerable medium bombers, which immediately followed the Typhoons.

Thirty-six Marauders were to bomb Amiens/Glisy airfield at 1100 hours and another thirty-six Marauders the airfield of Poix at 1150 hours. Poix again was the target of twelve RAF B-25 Mitchell medium bombers at 1244 hours.* All formations were to be escorted by RAF Spitfires.

Finally, at approximately the same time as the Fortress formations would leave the English coast in the late afternoon, an attack on Bryas-Sud, near Saint Pol, was to be made by thirty-six Marauders.

When the heavy bomber crews were enjoying a day's respite after their ordeal on the Schweinfurt mission, planning took place for an attack on August 19. It was to be only a short mission, with targets just inside the enemy occupied countries of Belgium and Holland.

A first indication that a mission was scheduled for the bomb groups was an incoming teletype message, giving advance information for the next operation. Important activities could be started on the various bases, as soon as the number of planes with their required bomb load was specified by headquarters of the bombardment wings. Other important information was the take-off time for the mission and the time over target—in this specific case, approximately 1500 and 1800 hours, respectively.

---

*The Americans used British Summer Time, one hour behind that being used by the Germans. British Summer Time will be the time quoted in this book, unless otherwise noted.

Finally, a detailed field order came out, giving minute details about formations, group and wing assemblies, bomb loads, and many other important details.

Especially at Ridgewell, where the hard-hit 381st Bomb Group was stationed, there was disbelief when the crews were summoned to the briefing room. Scheduled to fly as lead navigator was 1st Lt. Leonard L. Spivey. He recalls:

> I believe it was Colonel Nazzaro, our group commanding officer, at the briefing on the 19th who said words to the effect, "We have to show the Germans we are not knocked out, that we still have airplanes to fly, and that we can fly right back over and bomb them again." This was probably done in response to the puzzlement displayed by some of the aircrew; how could we fly another mission so soon with a third of the group's airplanes gone and with many of those surviving in no condition to get off the ground?
>
> Immediately after the briefing, Colonel Nazzaro came to me. He knew I had been to Schweinfurt and must have noticed my tiredness or maybe a glassy-eyed look that one gets from continuous combat. I distinctly remember him simply saying to me, "The war must go on." I assume it was either the Colonel or Major Ingenhutt, the commanding officer of the 535th Squadron, who assigned me to fly that day with Orlo Koenig leading our group. I had flown on the Schweinfurt mission as navigator with 1st Lt. Frank Chapman leading the 535th Bomb Squadron. The air battles with the fighters were so long-lasting, both in and out bound. I expended 2,700 rounds of .50-caliber ammunition besides trying to track position and maintain a log. Standing ankle deep in shells and swinging the guns on both sides of my compartment can be very tiring at an altitude of 20,000 feet.

On other airfields, a different mood prevailed—for example, on Molesworth, home of the 303rd Bomb Group, where later that evening pilot Robert L. Mattison wrote to his wife: "I started this letter, then went on a raid which was supposed to be what we call a 'milk run'—just a fast stab into the Low Lands—drop on a fighter field—and right out again. Everyone around was eager to go on it. Our two engineering officers got permission to ride and one of them went with me."

These two engineering officers were Capt. William F. Neff and 1st Lt. Louis T. Moffatt. The latter had submitted an official request to go on a mission "to observe aircraft and engine performance on extended high-altitude flights and to observe what troubles are encountered with oxygen systems and electrically heated clothing." The permission was duly granted and Moffatt boarded 1st Lt. James S. Nix's B-17 for the ride. We will meet both Robert Mattison and Louis Moffatt again later.

Most crew loading lists of the different bomb groups show that passengers went along. Staff officers from wing or Bomber Command headquarters, flight surgeons, other ground officers, and even fighter pilots were among those listed.

Some, like Moffatt, were motivated by operational reasons for taking part in some missions. For several others, it was probably the Air Medal, presented to an individual after five combat missions, which tempted them to take part. Apart from both engineering officers already mentioned above, here are some other examples of the passengers that went along. Major William M. Jackson, a flight surgeon from the headquarters of Eighth Air Force Bomber Command, flew aboard *Oklahoma Okie* of the 91st Bomb Group. Major Louis Novak, the flight surgeon of the 351st Bomb Group, flew on *Sharon Ann* of his group. Two fighter pilots, 2nd Lt. Joel W. McPherson and 2nd Lt. John H. Walter of the not-yet-operational 352nd Fighter Group boarded *Belle of the Bayous* and *Lucifer Jr*, also of the 351st Bomb Group.

First Lieutenant Bernard A. Ehrenreich, the public-relations officer of the 96th Bomb Group, was to get a firsthand story in *Dry Run III* of his group. Besides these, there were many other colonels and lieutenant colonels, mostly from wing or Bomber Command headquarters, who boarded B-17s on various airfields. One of these was Col. James E. Travis, the executive officer of the 403rd Provisional Combat Wing, who was to fly in 96th Bomb Group's *Black Heart Jr*.

The 1st Bombardment Wing was to put up two combat wing formations. The first was the 102nd Combat Wing, consisting of fifty-eight B-17s of the 92nd, 305th, and 306th Bomb Groups. The primary target for this combat wing was the Brussels/Evere airfield and the adjoining aircraft factory in Belgium.[*]

Besides being the prewar civilian airport for Brussels, Evere airfield was also used by the Belgian Air Force during its mobilization and the ensuing weeks of war in May 1940. Not only the airfield was of importance in these days, but also the neighboring maintenance and construction works of SABCA (Société Anonyme Belge de Constructions Aéronautiques) were

---

[*]Where applicable, the geographical names throughout the book are in English. Thus, for example, Flushing for Vlissingen and Hook of Holland for Hoek van Holland.

noticable. After the German capture of Belgium, work was started on a new airfield, Melsbroek, only a stone's throw away from Evere, and connected with it by taxi tracks. In the end, Melsbroek became even larger than Evere. The SABCA works were transformed by the Germans into a *Frontreparaturbetrieb*, an aircraft repair factory, called Erla VI, part of the Erla Maschinenwerke GmbH from Leipzig. Here repairs were performed on twin-engine German planes, like the Heinkel 111 and Messerschmitt 110.

As the target for the August 19, 1943, mission was Brussels/Evere and its aircraft factory, the intention was obviously to hit German repair capacity instead of the *Luftwaffe's* operational units stationed on Melsbroek.

The secondary target for the 102nd Combat Wing, to be attacked in case the primary target was missed for whatever reason, was the small Flushing airfield in Holland. Situated about one kilometer north of Flushing near the hamlet of West-Souburg, on the western bank of the canal through Walcheren Island, the airfield was established in 1939 by the Royal Netherlands Air Force and was used for pilot training. After the German invasion and subsequent Dutch surrender in May 1940, the *Luftwaffe* took over the airfield and used it as a base for some of their Messerschmitt 109 fighters during the Battle of Britain in the summer months of 1940. Its real operational use was discontinued in 1942, probably because of its proximity to the Dutch coast and its consequent vulnerability for "hit-and-run" attacks by enemy fighters and bombers. Since that time, it was only used as an emergency strip by the *Luftwaffe*.

The second combat wing to be put up by the 1st Bombardment Wing was the 103rd Composite Combat Wing, comprising sixty-seven B-17s of no fewer than six bomb groups, namely the 91st, 303rd, 351st, 379th, 381st, and 384th. Primary target for this wing was the Gilze-Rijen airfield, situated between Breda and Tilburg in Holland.

The heather between the villages Gilze and Rijen already saw its first military airplane in August 1913, when it landed there after reconnaissance flights during maneuvers. Early in 1937, serious effort was undertaken to develop the strip into a full-size military airfield. When the war for the Dutch started in May 1940, all work on runways had been completed; only the buildings had to be erected. The German occupiers immediately took this work to hand, and already, early in September 1940, the first German bombers landed on the field and started using it as their home base. Heinkels 111s of II./KG 26 and Junkers 88s of II./KG 30 were a familiar sight for the people around Gilze-Rijen, when they took off for their missions to England until May 1941.[*] New occupants eventu-

---

[*] For a basic explanation of the annotation of German units, see Appendix B.

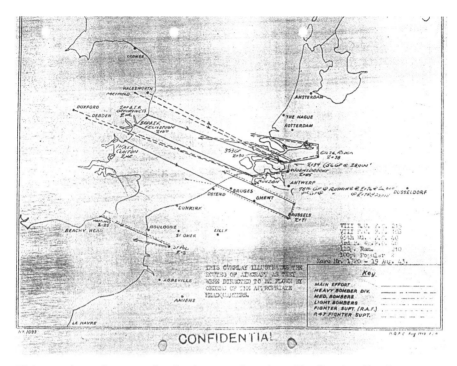

This map shows the routes for the three combat wings. The first, heading for Brussels, left Clacton at zero-hour. The second, flying to Gilze-Rijen, left Orfordness at the same time. The third, heading for Woensdrecht, left the English coast at Felixstowe fifty minutes later. At the bottom of the map, the diversion attack on Bryas-Sud, near St. Pol, at zero-minus 5 is indicated. Also shown are the bases and routes of the four American fighter groups that provided escort to the B-17s.

ally were Dornier 217 bombers and their crews of I./KG 2, III./KG 2, and II./KG 40, who also regularly bombed England or dropped mines near British harbors. However, not only bombers operated from Gilze-Rijen; Messerschmitt 110 night-fighters of III./NJG 1 were stationed here and wrought havoc among Royal Air Force crews over southern Holland and Belgium.

Last but not least, single-engine dayfighter units frequently used the field, as they were ordered around by a *Jagdführer* ("fighter controller") to different bases, to be as well positioned as possible to counter intruding American bomber formations.

It is clear that Gilze-Rijen was one of the main German airfields in Holland at the time, and its destruction by the Americans, if achieved, would certainly disrupt many important round-the-clock German flying activities. The 103rd Composite Wing did not have a designated secondary target.

In all, the 1st Bombardment Wing was to put up 125 Fortresses from nine different bomb groups in two combat wing formations.

The 4th Bombardment Wing, with the major part of its combat force still in North Africa after the shuttle mission to Regensburg, was to put up one single composite combat wing, the 402nd, consisting of forty-five B-17s of seven bomb groups: the 94th, 95th, 96th, 100th, 385th, 388th, and 390th.

The primary target for this wing was the Woensdrecht airfield, situated almost on the Dutch-Belgian border, about twenty-five kilometers north of Antwerp, the principal Belgian port. The history of this airfield started in 1934, when just under forty acres of land were used by a civilian gliding club. Now and then, the Dutch Air Force used it during maneuvers, but it was the Germans who really turned it into an airfield. Within a few months, in the summer of 1940, they had constructed a real operational fighter base. Me 109s of JG 3 and JG 52 and later the FW 190s of JG 1 used it as their base. It was of considerable value for the Germans, although less important than Gilze-Rijen. The latter became the assigned secondary target for the 402nd Combat Wing.

It was planned that the first two combat wings would depart the coast of England at so-called "zero hour" (1720 hours) and proceed to their targets at Brussels/Evere and Gilze-Rijen. The third force was to depart from England at zero hour plus fifty minutes and proceed to Woensdrecht. It was hoped that the attacks at the airfields at Brussels and Gilze-Rijen would damage them sufficiently so that they would be unable to launch fighters and that those in the wide area of Woensdrecht would be forced to choose that airfield for refuelling and re-arming, just prior being attacked.

Each of the three combat wings was assigned a part of the available fighters as escort.

The 102nd Combat Wing, destined for Brussels/Evere, was to have RAF fighters protecting it. Near Ostend, forty-one Spitfires were to make rendezvous with the B-17s and escort them to the target area. Here they were to be relieved by another seventy-three Spitfires, which would escort the bombers until they left hostile airspace.

The 103rd Composite Combat Wing, bombing Gilze-Rijen, was assigned American fighters. The 353rd Fighter Group, with forty-two P-47s was to act as penetration and target escort. The 56th Fighter Group, with fifty-one P-47s, as target and withdrawal escort.

The 402nd Composite Combat Wing, flying to Woensdrecht, was also assigned American fighters. Here the 4th Fighter Group acted as penetration and target escort and the 78th Fighter Group as target and withdrawal escort, with forty-eight and forty-nine Thunderbolts, respectively.

Although the majestic formations of American bombers, with their white contrails, were huge morale boosters for the civilians in the occupied countries, their appearance also had brought suffering among them. Various bomb groups had been assigned targets in the occupied countries earlier in the war. However, the accuracy of their bombing in some instances had left much to be desired.

On March 31, 1943, the bombs of two bomb groups hit residential areas, instead of harbor installations, in Rotterdam and resulted in more than 400 civilians casualties and much damage to civilian property. The Belgians had recent bad experiences with the American Eighth Air Force trying to hit Erla works in Mortsel, a suburb of Antwerp. On April 5, six bomb groups unloaded their bombs over this aircraft repair facility. Poor bombing resulted in more than 900 civilian casualties and no damage to the works.

Amsterdam was hit heavily on July 17, when two bomb groups on their first mission again hit residential areas, instead of the Fokker aircraft factory. More than 180 civilians died.

Finally, Flushing had received part of the bombs intended for its airfield only four days before this day's mission, on August 15. Just like on the nineteenth, Brussels/Evere was the primary target that day, and the airfield near Flushing was the secondary target. However, clouds hid the primary, and the bombers turned for Flushing. A large proportion of bombs hit the target, but a number of bombs in a suburb caused the loss of forty-one civilian lives. It is interesting to note that damage assessment in England in this instance was inaccurate, results were classified as "poor," and therefore the airfield was again on the mission list on the nineteenth. However, the Germans had noted that the airfield was "heavily damaged" by the bombs, and this, together with its already inactive status, made the efforts that the Americans would undertake on the nineteenth pointless. Such are the fortunes of war.

Of course, the Germans made a large propaganda effort in order to exploit these mishaps of the American air force, but generally, the people in the Low Countries were more than happy to see the Americans overhead. They were a sign of the oncoming liberation.

As a precautionary measure against friendly civilian casualties, it was explicitly stated in all field orders for American bomb groups that in no case would indiscriminate bombing be allowed over the Low Countries. The target had to be identified at all times. Strict obedience to this rule would cost American lives on August 19.

CHAPTER 3

Diversionary Attacks over France

AMIENS-GLISY AIRFIELD

The first aerial activity of the day, a fighter sweep, was conducted by twenty-four Typhoons of 183, 197, and 486 Squadrons. They left Tangmere at 1032 hours to carry out their sweep over Bernay and Beaumont-le-Roger. After crossing the French coast near Trouville, the wing had to turn back because of solid cloud cover with no breaks. As the weather conditions were clearer to the west, the wing then carried out an uneventful sweep over the area around Caen and Bayeux in Normandy before returning to England.

The second sweep left England one minute later, at 1033 hours. Again twenty-four Typhoons, of 174, 175, and 245 Squadrons, left Lydd for a sweep over the Ault, Poix, and Amiens area. 245 Squadron lost the wing formation in a sea fog and returned early. The remainder carried out an uneventful sweep, without observing any enemy aircraft. For one of the pilots of 174 Squadron, however, there was plenty of excitement. The engine of Pilot Officer O'Callaghan's Typhoon cut out during the return journey, some ten miles off the French coast at Le Touquet. O'Callaghan had no other option than to bail out over the Channel. He managed to climb in his dinghy, and after his location was reported by other pilots, a Walrus seaplane of the Air-Sea Rescue picked him up and returned him safely to England.

Where these first two sweeps were largely uneventful, this would not be the case for the third. At 1057 hours, nineteen Typhoons of 181, 182, and 247 Squadrons left Biggin Hill to sweep the Amiens, Poix, and Berck area, led by Flight Lt. W. H. "Bill" Ireson of 182 Squadron. In 1995, Ireson clearly recalled the events leading up to the mission:

> Although my flying log book contains only the bare essentials of this day (as every other day does also), I remember this operation distinctly for the following reasons:
>
> [1] the operation (a fighter sweep) was not the normal operation for Typhoons of this wing during 1943;

17

[2] it was an event for a wing to be led by a mere flight lieutenant as it would normally be a wing commander or senior squadron leader who performed that duty;

[3] it is hardly a recommendation for a leader of six aircraft of his own squadron and two further squadrons to lose half of his own command in battle.

Our Typhoon wing normally operated on the basis of one squadron with bombs for dive-bombing operations, escorted by the other two squadrons as fighter cover. Each squadron took turns either as bomber or escort duties. On this occasion, the three squadrons flew as a wing at 10,000-plus feet and went over at that height, rather than at low level climbing steeply some ten miles from the coast to 10,000 feet in an endeavour to surprise the enemy by being under the radar scan until the last moment. On this operation, the idea was to let everyone on the enemy side know that we were coming and to provoke some enemy fighter reaction and to engage them for distraction purposes to aid the main force.

This done, the idea was to engage and try to disperse the enemy force and so make sure it had to refuel early and give the main force some relief. The object therefore was not so much to commit the wing to a "life and death" struggle and possibly lose one's own force, but generally to make a very general nuisance of oneself!!

The squadron commander of 182 Squadron had been shot down and killed over Dunkirk just before (I was leading the second flight on that occasion) and had not been replaced. Thus I was temporarily in charge of the squadron. The squadron commanders of the other two units had very recently been posted to other jobs and their replacements were no doubt very fine pilots (per se), but had been on non-operational jobs in recent times and thus felt not able to take on leading the wing so early in their appointment as operational squadron commanders. Hence, as I was the senior flight commander in the wing, I got the job!!

Ireson's wing crossed the French coast at 13,000 feet near Ault, flying on to Poix. Then approximately thirty to forty FW 190s were sighted approaching Amiens 4,000 to 5,000 feet below. The wing then climbed in an endeavor the get into the sun and at the same time overhaul the enemy aircraft. The Germans, however, must have sighted them too, for they also climbed, and a fight ensued with only 800 feet of altitude in advantage of

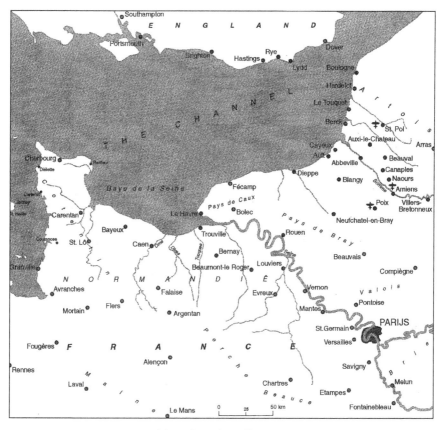

Map of northern France.

the Typhoons. Soon after the fight broke out, Ireson called over the radio for the wing to withdraw. Proper contact was not made and 181 and 247 Squadron left the area independently, but unscathed. A worse fate befell Ireson's own 182 Squadron. It had contributed two flights of three planes each to the mission. Ireson led Red Flight, Flight Lt. Geoffrey Ball Blue Flight. The latter was heard to say that he had shot down an enemy aircraft and was following it down, a cardinal sin in air-to-air combat. Ireson then withdrew his Red Flight over Cayeux and returned to England. Then Ball came back on the radio, saying that he was about to crashland. Nothing further was heard from him, or from Flight Officer Fraleigh and Flight Sergeant Dench, the other members of his Blue flight, who had followed him down. The squadron's operational record book notes: "The loss of these three pilots was a great blow to the squadron, as they were all fine types and excellent pilots. It is hoped that some of them may have landed safely in

Typhoon XM-K of 182 Squadron. Most probably, this was EK195, which served in the squadron in the summer of 1943. DOUG CASTLE

enemy territory. F/Lt Ball had only been with the squadron a short time, but had impressed everyone with his efficiency and dash. The squadron have now only three servicable aircraft, and it is hoped that replacements will arrive quickly."

Blue Flight's three pilots had run into II./JG 26. *Leutnant* Heinemann of its 4th Staffel claimed a Typhoon at 1224 hours one kilometer southeast of Canaples. *Leutnant* Hoppe of the same unit claimed a second and a third Typhoon, one at 1225 hours fifteen kilometers north of Amiens, the other at 1231 hours three to five kilometers northwest of Blangy. (Both German pilots were killed in action before year's end. Heinemann fell on September 4, Hoppe on December 1.) Flight Lieutenant G. F. Ball went down, was made prisoner of war, and spent the rest of the war in Stalag Luft III. Flight Sergeant Ronald L. H. Dench also came down in the Amiens area. He recalls:

We were flying at 12,000 feet, I believe, when Tangmere radar reported thirty plus enemy aircraft approaching us head-on. Bill Ireson climbed the squadron until we sighted the mass of FW 190s, then put our six aircraft into a defensive circle. One FW 190, acting, I believe, as bait to break our defensive circle, went into a steep dive. Geoff Ball immediately followed it, followed by myself and Joe Fraleigh. I fired a short burst at another FW 190 and lost sight of

Geoff Ball. I was searching for the rest of the wing when the aircraft was struck by a burst of cannon fire which stopped the engine. I jettisoned the hood, undid the harness, and baled out. My canopy opened and I found I was being circled by the FW 190 which had shot me down. He followed me until I was on the ground and, as I made for some woods, he fired a burst which missed me.

Dench managed to evade the Germans and return to England with the help of the French underground. (Dench finally reached Gibraltar three months after being shot down, on November 19, and returned to his squadron.) Flight Officer Manley I. Fraleigh, a Canadian from Ontario, flying in a Typhoon that was borrowed from 181 Squadron, was not so lucky. He was killed and was buried in the communal cemetery in Beauval.

Flight Lieutenant Ireson reflects about the events:

It was my intention to aim to get the leaders of the German formation with the intention of causing chaos among those following, as I was aware that many of the German units at this stage of the war contained many new pilots (as did ours) and that if they saw their leaders under attack they might panic and so cause the whole formation to split. This indeed happened and many in the group very smartly dived vertically away from the formation at high speed. At this stage, I called up the other two squadrons and invited them down to join in the fray but I can only surmise that the message did not get through or, if it did, they did not get the impact of the message through lack of experience.

I was not prepared for any squadron to follow the Germans down at that stage as they had dispersed to all quarters which had been the prime aim. Unfortunately, Geoff Ball, Blue Flight commander, must have been keen to see what damage he had done and went down with the general German melee and took Fraleigh and Dench with him, with unfortunate results. They were all of them great fellows and I can't keep thinking it was unneccessary that they were put in the position of being shot down.

The next Allied formation to appear over northern France, in advance of the bombers still yet to come, was the so-called target forward support. At 1036 hours, twenty-four Spitfires of 303 and 316 (Polish) Squadrons, commanded by Wing Cmdr. A. Gabszevicz, left Northolt and on approaching Amiens were warned of enemy aircraft to the north. Then five or six FW 190s were engaged by 316 Squadron, which was then in turn attacked by

Typhoons of 182 Squadron ready for take-off. W. H. IRESON

Personnel of 182 Squadron posing with a Typhoon in July 1943. Four of the pilots took part in the ill-fated fighter sweep to Amiens on August 19. Standing third from left is Flight Officer Calder, and fourth from left is Flight Lieutenant Ireson, who also led the wing that fateful day. Seated on the left is Flight Sergeant Dench, who was shot down and evaded back to England, and in the center is Flight Officer Fraleigh, who was killed. W. H. IRESON

some twenty FW 190s. Combats ensued, with the result that the Polish pilots claimed no less than six enemy aircraft destroyed and three damaged. 303 Squadron remained above and did not join in the action. During the combats, at a time when 316 Squadron was split up and busily engaged, one of its pilots, Flight Off. Andrzej Prochnicki, by means of his radio called for assistance, saying that he was being attacked by four or five FW 190s. He subsequently failed to return from the mission, but it was believed that he had later given a "Mayday." Aircraft of the wing, immediately after they had refuelled after the mission, took off again to search for the missing pilot. They located an occupied dinghy just off the French coast and this pilot was ultimately picked up by a Walrus. The unit was confident that they had found Prochnicki, but it was later ascertained that this was a pilot of 131 Squadron. The disappointment on Northolt must have been great and early next morning, at 0550 hours, four aircraft took off again to search the Channel in the Boulogne-Le Touquet area for their squadron mate. Again, the search proved without avail. Unknown to those at Northolt, Prochnicki had been killed during his fight with the FW 190s. He crashed near Naours, north of Amiens, and was buried there. After the war he was buried in the Polish Military Cemetery in Grainville-Langannerie in the Calvados Department. The German unit that was involved was most probably again JG 26. However, the Polish claim of six enemy fighters destroyed seems exaggerated. One of the pilots of JG 26, *Oberleutnant* Johannes Meyer of the 10th Staffel was killed in the crash of his FW 190 near Villers-Bretonneux. *Unteroffizier* Martin Günther of the 4th Staffel was wounded when he was shot down near Amiens in his FW 190. Finally, a battle-damaged FW 190 of the 6th Staffel, was belly-landed by its pilot on Poix airfield.

Leutnant Helmut Hoppe of 2./JG 26 shot down two Typhoons of 182 Squadron. PETER CRUMP VIA DONALD L. CALDWELL

Then the American bombers made their way to Amiens/Glisy. Thirty-six B-26s of the 323rd Bomb Group, loaded with 351 300-pound general-purpose bombs, took off from Earls Colne. Their fighter escort, provided by the Royal Air Force, was strong— and not without reason. Forty-eight Spitfires of 132, 130, 234, and 602

Flight Off. Andrzej Prochnicki of 316 (Polish) Squadron posing next to Spitfire AB508 at Northolt in May 1943. Prochnicki was killed in action on August 19. AB508 was flown on that same mission by Warrant Off. S. Wojcik. It was lost three days later when it was shot down by FW 190s near Rouen, France. POLISH INSTITUTE AND SIKORSKY MUSEUM

Oberleutnant Johannes Meyer of 10./JG 26. He was shot down and killed in action during combat with Spitfires over northern France.
MILITÄRARCHIV FREIBURG

Squadrons were flying close escort, twenty-two Spits of 131 and 504 Squadrons were escort cover, and twenty-four Spits of 341 and 485 Squadrons were high cover. Rendezvous was accomplished over Rye at 1100 hours, and an uneventful flight to the target area took place. Here heavy flak greeted the formation and a swarm of FW 190s attacked the Marauder force. Bombs were dropped with results reported as "good." Numerous combats took place in the target area and during the return flight to England. The close escort squadrons claimed three FW 190s damaged, for two Spits damaged on their own side. The escort cover squadrons claimed one FW 190 damaged. The high cover squadrons claimed an Me 109 destroyed, a FW 190 probably destroyed, and one Me 109 and four FW 190s damaged.

Gunners aboard the Marauders claimed one FW 190 destroyed and three probably destroyed. Seven of the group's aircraft received battle damage, two made emergency landings, and one crash-landed on Earls Colne. Two of the B-26 gunners, Sgt. John K. Burns and Sgt. Adam W. Glen, returned wounded.

POIX AIRFIELD

At 1150 hours, thirty-five Spitfires of 118, 402, and 416 Squadrons (close escort) from Tangmere, twenty Spits of 66 and 151 Squadrons (escort cover) from Kenley, and twenty-four Spits of 129 and 222 Squadrons (high cover) from Hornchurch made rendezvous over Rye with thirty-six Marauders of the 387th Bomb Group, from Chipping Ongar. The formation flew to the target, which was attacked by all but one of the Marauders, dropping 350 300-pound general-purpose bombs, with good results. Only two Me 109s were sighted by the escort, but not attacked. All aircraft returned safely to base.

A second attack was conducted by the Royal Air Force. At 1244 hours, thirty-five Spitfires of 401, 411, and 412 Squadrons (close escort) from Stapelhurst, twenty-four Spits of 41 and 91 Squadrons (escort cover) from Tangmere, and twenty-three Spits of 331 and 332 Squadrons (high cover) from North Weald made rendezvous over Rye with twelve Mitchells of 320 (Dutch) Squadron, which had taken off from Foulsham. Over the target, twenty-six 500-pound general-purpose bombs were dropped. Bursts were observed in the north and south dispersals and the center of the airfield. No enemy aircraft were encountered and all aircraft returned safely.

The next operation over northern France was again a fighter sweep, conducted by twenty-four Spitfires of 403 and 421 Squadrons. They left Lashenden at 1245 hours and carried out a patrol over the Hardelot-Abbeville area. Twelve Me 109s were encountered south of Abbeville, and although they split up when attacked, Flight Lt. A. C. Coles of 403 Squadron destroyed one. He reported:

> Not hearing instructions to break off, I followed a pair of Me 109s down, and as we approached them from behind, they half-rolled and started to go down. Two broke away to the starboard and continued in a diving turn to starboard. At this time, Blue 3 and I were to the starboard side of our formation and we swung around and down after these two. I passed Blue 3 and opened fire on one Me 109 at about 600 yards. I believe I made a strike on the engine but continued after him, opening again at approximately 300 to 400 yards. I saw numerous bursts on the cockpit and rear of the engine. I continued firing bursts to a fairly low height. The last bursts showed heavy strikes on and around the cockpit and several small pieces flew off the plane. He continued in a shallow diving turn, striking the ground at an angle across a road and leaving a sheet of flame for 100 to 150 yards.

Coles's victim was most probably *Unteroffizier* Heinz Köckler of II./JG 2, who was killed in the crash of his Me 109 near Auxi-le-Chateau. Another

Hauptmann Johannes Naumann, the
Gruppenkommandeur of II./JG 26.
Flight Sgt. R. K. Parry of 131
Squadron was his twenty-second
combat victory. MICHAEL MEYER VIA
DONALD L. CALDWELL

Me 109 was damaged by Flight Off. A.
E. Fleming of 421 Squadron. This,
however, was not without loss for the
Royal Air Force. F. C. Joyce, a Canadian of 421 Squadron, who only a few
hours before take-off had been noti-
fied of his commission to pilot officer,
was last seen coming out over the
Somme estuary, flying in his Spitfire
MA453. Not being able to make it
back to England, he bailed out and
was picked up by the Germans. He
spent the rest of the war as a prisoner
of war in Stalag Luft IV. All others
returned safely to their bases.

BRYAS-SUD AIRFIELD

The final operation of the day over
northern France was scheduled to
coincide with the Fortress operations
over Holland. Thirty-six B-26s of the
322nd Bomb Group took off from
Andrews Field to bomb the Bryas-Sud
landing ground near Saint Pol. Forty-
three Spitfires of 66, 131, 165, and 504 Squadrons (close escort) and twenty-
four Spitfires of 65 and 122 Squadrons (high cover) made rendezvous over
Hastings with the Marauders. Over the target area, a solid cloud cover was
encountered, so the bombs were not dropped and the trip had been in vain.
More than thirty FW 190s and Me 109s that attempted to attack the bombers
were sighted as the formation recrossed the French coast. These were
engaged by the high cover squadrons. As a result of this combat, one
FW 190 was claimed destroyed by Flight Lieutenant Heap of 65 Squadron
and another damaged. The Germans scored a success, too. The operational
record book of 131 Squadron relates:

> On the way back, when at 12,000 feet, six FW 190s from Boulogne
> direction bounced yellow section of the formation led by W/Cdr
> Malfroy. One aircraft was seen going down in flames and it was sub-
> sequently learned that it was F/Sgt Parry. He had been hit in the
> port wing and the fuselage by cannon shells and the Spit caught

fire. He managed to keep the aircraft straight and level, and flew it two thirds of the way back over the Channel before the engine "packed up" altogether and he baled out off Dungeness, to be picked up safely by a vessel of the Dover Patrol. A "shaky do" for all of us, but as Parry himself kept his head and did the right things at the right times, everything went satisfactorily. F/Sgt Turnbull flew to Hawkinge in the Tiger Moth to fetch him back, none the worse for the experience.

Flight Sergeant R. K. Parry had been the victim of experienced *Hauptmann* Johannes Naumann. He was the new *Gruppenkommandeur* (commanding officer) of II./JG 26 after *Major* Wilhelm-Ferdinand Galland, the brother of famous Adolf Galland, had been killed in action two days earlier. Parry's Spitfire was his twenty-second combat victory. (Naumann remained in command of the unit until June 23, 1944, when he was wounded after bailing out of his aircraft after it was hit by Allied flak over Normandy.)

It is now time to look at the exploits of the heavy bombers over Belgium and Holland.

An FW 190 of JG 26 on Wevelghem in March 1943. Note the distinctive yellow band around the Cowling. The pilot is *Feldwebel* Werner Möszner. WERNER MÖSZNER

CHAPTER 4

Flushing

The 102nd Combat Wing was led by Col. Delmar E. Wilson in B-17F 42-30242 *Lallah-V III* of the 305th Bomb Group. It was piloted by 1st Lt. F. Robert Spitznagel. The lead navigator and bombardier were 2nd Lt. Karl H. Brauer and 1st Lt. Robert D. Metcalf.

The 305th Bomb Group took off from Chelveston and proceeded to make the briefed assembly with the other two groups of the combat wing over Thurleigh, base of the 306th Bomb Group, at 1610 hours. However, an unpredicted cloud layer forced them to spend an extra minute in the climb and they arrived over Thurleigh at 1611 hours. First, the high group, the 92nd Bomb Group, was sighted ahead and above. Then the low group, the 306th Bomb Group, was seen behind, below the cloud level.

B-17F 42-29894, the lead ship of the 306th Bomb Group, was flown by Capt. Thomas F. Witt. His navigator, Capt. George D. Bennett, reported:

> Our group took off at 1535 hours for primary target at Brussels, Belgium. The group had a little difficulty in assembling. We crossed the field at 5,500 feet at 1608 hours, going under a cloud layer. We did not see the lead group, and being about two minutes early, we turned to Wellingborough on our way to Northampton. We arrived at Northampton at 1618 hours at 5,600 feet and saw the 305th and 92nd Bomb Groups. Course was set for Banbury, and the group climbed through the clouds, breaking out at 7,500 feet. The 305th Bomb Group fired a flare and we fell in behind them. At 1628 hours, we arrived at Banbury at 9,000 feet and set course for Newbury.

Leading the nineteen aircraft of the 92nd Bomb Group from Alconbury was Maj. McGehee Word, Jr., in B-17F 42-30231, piloted by 1st Lt. Arthur M. Stone. He reported:

> The 92nd Bomb Group flew to the assembly point at 9,400 feet, which was 2,400 feet above the scheduled altitude. This change was made because of a well-developed cloud layer at the scheduled

altitude. At the assembly point, Thurleigh, the lead group of the combat wing formation, was observed beneath the clouds, and so our group flew the scheduled route and waited for the lead group to climb above the clouds. The lead group was observed to penetrate the layer at Northampton, and a successful rendezvous was accomplished three miles west of Oxford at 1635 hours at 10,500 feet. From that point on, the 92nd Bomb Group flew high group and followed the combat wing leader.

No problems so far for the 102nd Combat Wing. The headquarters of the First Bombardment Wing later reported: "The combat wing assembly was not achieved as briefed; however, due to good leadership on the part of the lead group, assembly was accomplished on the wing assembly line, and

The lead crew of the 102nd Combat Wing attacking Flushing. Back row, left to right: 2nd Lt. Karl H. Brauer (navigator), 1st Lt. F. Robert Spitznagel (pilot), 2nd Lt. Samuel R. Johnson (copilot, not on mission), 1st Lt. Robert D. Metcalf (bombardier). Front row, left to right: Staff Sgt Frank Rollow (waist gunner, not on mission), Staff Sgt. Jesse M. Pogue (ball turret gunner), Tech Sgt. John L. Guminey (radio operator), Tech Sgt. Timothy Riordan (top turret gunner), Staff Sgt. Harold Hambleton (waist gunner, not on mission), Staff Sgt. Willis G. Rose (tail gunner, flew right waist gun). F. ROBERT SPITZNAGEL

the combat wing, upon arriving at the point of departure on the English Coast, was in good battle formation."

The flight over the North Sea was routine. Only two B-17s, both of the 92nd Bomb Group, aborted the mission. First, B-17F 42-3105 turned back because the ball turret gunner was unable to turn the turret down and enter it in flight. Then, after approximately two hours of flight, the oil pressure on the number four engine of B-17F 42-30008 *Ready Teddy* dropped suddenly, and the engine began to smoke. The propeller was feathered, and the ship returned to Alconbury. The bombs aboard both aircraft were brought back. All scheduled ships of the 305th and 306th remained in their formations.

However, Colonel Wilson in the wing's lead ship was faced with a problem as the Belgian coast came near. The weather forecast had predicted the following cloud conditions for the route over the North Sea and over the target: "Patches of stratus at 2,000 feet over North Sea, becoming 3 to 5/10 cumulus [cloud cover] at 2,500 feet. Tops 3,500–4,000 feet over Continent. 2 to 3/10 patches of altocumulus decreasing to nil on continental coast. 3 to 5/10 cirrus at 25,000 to 30,000 feet." Visibility had been predicted as being at least 10 miles.

However, lead bombardier Robert D. Metcalf now had to report: "Pilot, co-pilot, two navigators, and I decided not to hit the primary target because of cloud cover. We turned left and made a ninety-second run on the secondary target."

A welcome sight for American bomber crews. A formation of twelve RAF Spitfires on their way to escort duties. TONY GAZE

Major Kaj Birksted, DFC, a Danish pilot serving in 331 (Norwegian) Squadron. He led the North Weald Wing on August 19. WERNER CHRISTIE

Despite all the fine predictions, total cloud cover had hidden the Evere aircraft factory and airfield at Brussels, just like four days before. As the field order had clearly stated that in no case was indiscriminate bombing allowed, course was set for the secondary target, the airfield near Flushing in Holland. Quick action and calculations followed aboard the lead ship of the wing. Terneuzen, just over the border in Holland, was chosen as the initial point for the attack on this secondary target.

While crossing the Belgian coast, and thus flying over enemy territory, no German fighter attacks were made on the 102nd Combat Wing. It was due to the effective fighter escort, provided by the Royal Air Force.

Part of this escort were forty-one Spitfires of the 303, 316, 331, and 332 Squadrons. The first two were Polish squadrons, the latter two Norwegian. Many of the pilots were flying their second sortie for the day, after the mission to France in the morning.

Major Kaj Birksted and twenty-two other pilots of the 331 and 332 Squadrons had departed Manston at 1725 hours. Birksted, a Danish pilot in a Norwegian squadron, reported:

> We made rendezvous five miles northeast of Ostend at 1743 hours and at 24,000 feet, Fortresses at 22,000 feet. I advised controller that whole target was covered with 10/10ths cloud, but Forts continued towards target until 1755 hours, turning north approximately near Sas van Gent, north of which free from cloud. On to Goes, then turned port out over Walcheren. We remained up sun of the Fortresses at 26/28,000 feet. When inside Knocke, 331 Squadron, at 28,000 feet, sighted fifteen Me 109s against cloud four miles to port heading towards Fortresses.

Leading 331 Squadron (Red 1) was Captain Martin Gran:

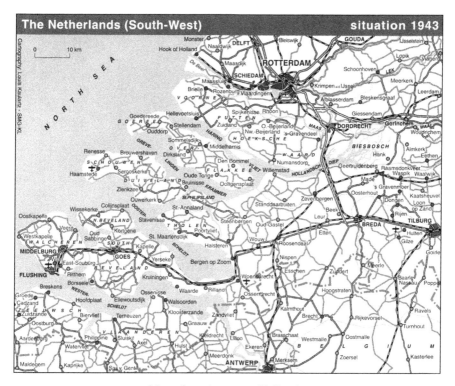

Map of southwestern Holland.

I reported enemy aircraft flying in the same direction and some 5,000 feet below us. I got permission to jump them and so led the Squadron down to attack. I picked out two Me 109s, flying line abreast, opening fire on the port one, giving one short burst at 300 yards range. I saw strikes and continued to close in and gave him several more bursts, seeing strikes on the engine, cockpit and both wings near the fuselage. He finally exploded in front of me, pieces flying off in all directions. I then turned starboard and attacked the other aircraft from 150 to 0 yards, giving a short burst and saw strikes on the port wing above the radiator, then turned away to avoid collision.

Gran's wingman was Sgt. Ragnar Dogger. He finished off this second Me 109: "I followed this enemy aircraft and closing in to very short range, about 150 to 0 yards, I fired from dead astern. I saw strikes in the left wing-root and left side of the fuselage, round the cockpit. A big piece blew off

Captain Martin Gran posing near a
331 (Norwegian) Squadron Spitfire.
Note the red, white, and blue colors
of the Norwegian flag on the spinner.
FORSVARSMUSEET

Sergeant Ragnard Dogger.
KRISTIAN NYERROD

and thick black smoke poured out. It flicked over and as I pulled away to
avoid collision I saw it spinning down, with black smoke pouring out, out of
control."

Lieutenant Nils Jorstad tells an almost similar story: "After the turn I
ended up on Red 1's starboard side, 500 yards away. I saw him open fire on
the port enemy aircraft and a great explosion. I picked out one of the starboard aircraft and opened fire from about 200 yards, about 15 degrees off
port. I gave one small burst and hit it in the port wing, root, and port side of
cockpit. A large explosion followed, it flicked left onto its back and went
down in a sort of spin; flames and black smoke pouring from it."

The fourth and last successful Norwegian fighter pilot was 2nd Lt. Knut
Bache, who had to make a long chase for his victory:

I followed Red 1 down and saw ten to twelve Me 109s flying toward
the coast. I picked out one Me 109 that was straggling about 1,000
yards behind the main formation, throttled right back and went
down in "S"-turns while he was diving gently. I came into position
dead astern of him at about 200 yards range and fired a two seconds
burst, observing a cannon hit followed by a small explosion on port

side of the cockpit. He carried on straight ahead and still diving gently, without taking any evasive action at all. I consider it likely that I either damaged the controls or wounded the pilot. I fired long bursts, but did not observe more than two more cannon hits, one in port wing root and one on starboard side of fuselage. I had difficulty in keeping my aircraft steady due to his slipstream when I closed in. Just when my cannon ammo was exhausted, I saw the hood of the enemy aircraft being jettisoned and pulling up in a very steep turn to port, saw it roll onto its back with white smoke issuing from it and the pilot bailing out.

Second Lt. Knut Bache. He was killed in action on May 7, 1944, near Pontoise, France. KRISTIAN NYERROD

The troubles for the Germans were not over yet. Major Birksted, himself still with the B-17s and observing the bounce from above, reported that "The remaining Huns which dove inland were jumped by one of the other three wings."

These other three wings that Birksted reported consisted of seventy-three Spitfires, which were provided by the 129, 222, 341, 403, 421, and 485 Squadrons. Here again, many pilots flew a second mission on the day.

Famous Wing Cmdr. Johnnie Johnson was leading 403 and 421 Squadrons. While 421 Squadron acted as top cover, 403 Squadron engaged the Germans. Flight Lieutenant Dean H. Dover, leading 403 Squadron, sighted the Me 109s:

> I dove down to port to attack. The gaggle of enemy aircraft split up and I selected one, the starboard one of three, closing in to attack to within 150 yards. I gave a one second burst and then my de-icing container blew up. I could not observe the results because of the fluid on the inside of my windscreen. I tried a further two seconds burst and then broke off the attack. Thirty to forty seconds later, I observed an enemy aircraft burning on the ground near the road east of Breskens.

Lieutenant Nils Jorstad sitting on the tail of a 331 (Norwegian) Squadron Spitfire.
FORSVARSMUSEET

Flight Lt. Tony Gaze of 129 Squadron, who also escorted the B-17s over Flushing. TONY GAZE

Another Me 109 was claimed destroyed by two pilots of 403 Squadron, Flight Officer Branagan and Flight Officer Dowding. The first reported: "I was behind another Me 109. I attacked him with a two second burst from 350 yards. It was also attacked by the wing commander and Flight Officer Dowding. I saw one parachute almost immediately afterward going into the water between approximately Nieuwe Sluis and Flushing."

Wing Commander Johnson observed two parachutes shortly after the encounter over the water south of Flushing and also the aircraft burning on the ground east of Breskens. Because there were no other engagements at the time in that area, both Me 109s were claimed destroyed. As we will see later, it is very likely that these chutes belonged to crewmembers of a B-17 of the 305th Bomb Group.

The Germans were still on the receiving end. Six Me 109s sighted north of Knocke were attacked by the 129 and 222 Squadrons, resulting in a claim of one destroyed by Wing Commander Compton and another one destroyed, shared by Flight Lieutenant Tripe and Flight Officer Hesselyn. Tripe reported about the violent end of his victim:

> As I was about to open fire, I saw strikes on his port wing and I realised that Blue 3 (Flight Officer Hesselyn) was also attacking. I opened fire from 300 yards astern, closing to 50 yards. The fuselage and belly of the enemy aircraft was a mass of flames and smoke, the starboard wing outboard of the cannon broke off and I had to push the stick hard forward to avoid collision. The enemy aircraft went down disintegrating and well on fire, the pilot did not bale out.

The Messerschmitts that the Spitfires had run in to, belonged to III./JG 1. The unit had taken off from its base in Leeuwarden earlier that afternoon and had then spend a few hours on Gilze-Rijen airfield. One of its pilots was experienced *Feldwebel* Hans Meissner, who recalled:

> I was leading the 9th Staffel, as Lt. Wintergerst had technical problems. Contact with the enemy was made in the area of Ostend. Our

Feldwebel Hans Meissner of 9./JG 1, who was shot down by a Spitfire and had to crash-land his Me 109 near Walsoorden. He was badly wounded and admitted to an Antwerp hospital. ROB W. DE VISSER

Gruppe split in two. Zuzic's Staffel and mine attacked from the right, the rest led by Olejnik from the left. The combat with the Spitfires began and I quickly lost Zuzic from sight. Spitfires came towards me. We were face to face and opened fire simultaneously. I was hit in the foot. My 109 was riddled but remained controllable and I escaped from the English. My aircraft would not make it back to Woensdrecht, so I found a field and made a belly landing. The aircraft bounced hard, the impact was very violent.

Hans Meissner had belly-landed his Me 109 19992 *Gelbe 12* near Walso-orden. For treatment of his wounds, he had to be admitted to the Antwerp hospital.

As already became apparent from the various British reports cited above, it had been a very costly affair for the German unit.

Oberleutnant Herwig Zuzic, the *Staffelkapitän* of the 8th Staffel, was killed in the crash of his Me 109 15367 *Schwarze 1*, near Zuidzande. According to German sources, he had collided with Me 109 15472 *Schwarze 8*, which made an emergency landing near Cadzand in turn, this pilot saving his life. It is,

Oberleutnant Herwig Zuzic, *Staffelkapitän* of 8./JG 1, climbing into the cockpit of his Me 109 G-6 15367 *Schwarze 1* on Leeuwarden airfield. Note the *Staffel* insignia, a dog urinating on a hat decorated with the British and American flags. The heart with number 7 and banner Lauser, underneath the cockpit, was Zuzic's personal insignia. He was killed flying this aircraft on August 19. ROB W. DE VISSER

Twenty-six-year-old *Oberleutnant* Herwig Zuzic, *Staffelkapitän* of 8./JG 1, seated in the center. He was killed on August 19. The other pilots are *Oberleutnant* Hardt and *Hauptmann* Luckenbach. ROB W. DE VISSER

however, more likely that both actually were victims of the Spitfires during the bounce. Another German fatality was *Leutnant* Horst Bork of the 9th Staffel. He crashed in his Me 109 20498 *Gelbe 3* near Philippine. Yet another German *Leutnant* lost his life. Hans-Joachim Niemeyer of the 9th Staffel came down east of Groede with his Me 109 20092 *Gelbe 11*. His mortal remains could not be recovered from the crash site, and a small memorial was erected over it. Finally, an unknown German pilot belly-landed Me 109 15612 of the 8th Staffel in the area, escaping unscathed himself. In all, actual German losses in the encounter were six Messerschmitts, with three pilots killed and one wounded in action. It is obvious that III./JG 1 posed no threat to the American bombers any more.

However, where the German *Luftwaffe* was not able to mount a concentrated attack on the bomber formations, the flak took its deadly toll. Up to the initial point over Terneuzen, only a few scattered bursts of flak were noticed and reported by the crews in the 102nd Combat Wing.

But around Flushing the four batteries of the Marine Flak Abteilung 810 were ready and waiting for them. The batteries, each with four 105mm guns as main armament, were situated to the north, east and west of Flushing; the fourth battery was posted near Breskens, on the other, southern, side of the Westerscheldt River.

Me 109 G-6 15472 *Schwarze 8* of 8./JG 1 "baking" on Leeuwarden airfield on a hot summer day in 1943, with its ground crew and pilot, *Unteroffizier* Einberger. The records do not indicate the pilot's name for the August 19 mission, when this aircraft was belly-landed near Cadzand. Note the *Staffel* insignia (the dog with the hat) and a personal insignia of the pilot underneath the cockpit. ROB W. DE VISSER

The final resting place of twenty-year-old *Leutnant* Horst Bork in the German Military Cemetery in Ysselsteyn in Holland. AUTHOR

Marine-Flak-Batterie West on the Nolledike near Flushing with its four 105mm guns.
The turrets were each covered with a fifteen-millimeter-thick steel plate. Note the
"anti-invasion" obstacles in front of the dike. BUNDESARCHIV KOBLENZ

Korvetten Kapitän Hans Köll, the commanding officer of Marine Flak
Abteilung 810, made this entry in his war diary:

1752 hours. Approaching engine noises are picked up in the direction 5–6 o'clock.*

The incoming formation, flying from 4 to 10 o'clock, is fired
upon by the North, East, and West batteries. It is out of reach for
the South battery.

The first volleys are well in the formation, which is now forced to
make a little course correction. A four-engine bomber receives a
direct hit and crashes in the Scheldt River at 3 o'clock.

The next volleys hit another four-engine bomber and a fighter,
both crash at 3 o'clock. Seven crewmembers bail out with their parachute. The formation flies a little to the north of the airfield and
after dropping about 500 bombs, it turns toward 10 o'clock. The
bombs hit the northern edge of the airfield and the village of
Souburg. The airfield receives only minor damage.

Total ammunition used: 185 rounds 105mm Flak.

---

*The Germans used the clock system to give quick reference to the approach of
enemy aircraft. Twelve o'clock in this particular case was due north. The Americans
used the clock system aboard their fighters and bombers; here, twelve o'clock was
the nose of the ship and six o'clock its tail.

One of the 105mm guns of *Marine-Flak-Batterie West*. This battery, together with two similar batteries to the north and east of Flushing, was credited with the destruction of *Lady Liberty*. BUNDESARCHIV KOBLENZ

Köll's unit thus claimed two bombers and a fighter shot down. In fact, it had been one B-17F, which was destroyed. However its demise was so violent, that it is easy to understand that the Germans thought it were at least two, or even three planes coming down.

The official report of the 305th Bomb Group has this entry on the event:

> Antiaircraft gun fire was encountered at the target (Flushing) at 1756 hours, 20,000 feet. It was meager, but very accurate. The bursts were black and several crews reported them as being larger than usual. All our aircraft received some damage from the flak. The only aircraft seen going down was our own 42-29807. It suffered a direct hit by flak in the waist section. This aircraft broke in two and each separate part fell tumbling down. This occurred on the bomb run at 1755 hours, at 20,000 feet. Three to four parachutes were seen.

The unfortunate crew was that of 1st Lt. Ralph R. Miller, flying in B-17F 42-29807 *Lady Liberty* of the 364th Bomb Squadron. The plane carried the fuselage code WF-O.

One of the crew to survive was Ralph Miller himself. Later, he wrote:

> August 19. All crewmembers were at their places in the ship waiting for the tower's instructions to taxi out for take-off—the target was

With all four engines running, B-17F 42-29807 *Lady Liberty* is ready to leave her hardstand on Chelveston, home of the 305th Bomb Group. ROGER V. MILLER

The crew of *Lady Liberty* posing on Chelveston. They were shot down by flak and crashed near Flushing on August 19. Back row, left to right: 2nd Lt. John F. Meade (copilot, KIA), 1st Lt. Ralph R. Miller (pilot, POW), 2nd Lt. Joseph M. McGinley (bombardier, KIA), 2nd Lt. Donald J. McGowan (navigator, KIA). Front row, left to right: Staff Sgt. Albert F. Miller (ball turret gunner, MIA), Tech Sgt. Bynum G. Crabtree (engineer, KIA), Staff Sgt. Edgar G. Lott (right waist gunner, MIA), Staff Sgt. Emil Radosevich (tail gunner, POW), Tech Sgt. Fulton F. Horn (radio operator, KIA). ROGER V. MILLER

Brussels, Belgium. All morning we had waited and it was now early afternoon. Weather ships had been reporting Brussels covered with clouds. We might have to take our secondary target, an airfield on the coast of Flushing, Holland. Meade and I were chatting in the pilot seats when the order came to taxi.

"John, I certainly am happy to have this milk-run for the thirteenth mission," I said, "It's so soothing to the nerves to have our fighters all the way, I don't mind the flak if we don't have to look at those fighters." John agreed but expressed his non-belief in superstition. Just two days before, we had returned safely from one of the greatest air battles ever fought: the first twin raids on Schweinfurt and Regensburg. All set, down the runway and throttling up to join the squadron in formation now seemed like old stuff, a new confidence had been born in us. Squadron joined with group, group with wing, and as wing joined with other wings, we were high over England, 21,000 feet, heading straight for Brussels.

What a rosy feeling it was to look out and see our own fighters dancing all around us and knowing that they would be there all the way. We did not expect to fire a single shot; they even sent a photographer along in the ship next to ours to get a picture of our bombs coming out. Many ground officers of the group that had

Second Lt. Donald J. McGowan at the port nose gun of *Lady Liberty*.
DEBBIE MILLER HUGHES

Second Lt. Joseph M. McGinley taking his turn at the port nose gun of *Lady Liberty*.
DEBBIE MILLER HUGHES

Staff Sgt. Emil Radosevich, the tail gunner, posing with the port waist gun of *Lady Liberty*. He miraculously survived the demise of the bomber. DEBBIE MILLER HUGHES

been able to talk operations into a ride had crowded into the planes—five of these and they would receive an Air Medal.

Brussels was covered by clouds, we saw the wings in front turning left toward Flushing Island. Boy, what a milk run, not an enemy fighter in sight!! Then only a few minutes passed before we saw the bombs dropping from the Wings far in front. In hardly any time McGinley on intercom, "Bomb bay doors open," moments later, "I.P., two minutes to target," then Rudy in the tail, "Flak, two bursts, six o'clock level," then McGinley again, "Thirty seconds to target".

At this moment, over the roar of the engines and in spite of the fact that my steel helmet pressed hard against my earphones, I heard a thunderous explosion. I did not think of it for at the same moment the plane lurched upward, and as automatic as formation flying can be, I threw the wheel and stick forward; they were as limp as anybody's dish rag. As I realized that I had no control, the ship flopped into a vertical dive. All engines sounded as if they were running away, the screams of the dive sounded like a mess of wild-cats. I jerked the throttles back, nothing happened; I tried to hit the

This picture was taken out of the right waist gun window of B-17F 42-29529 *Nora* of the 305th Bomb Group on August 19. The subject plane is B-17F 42-29807 *Lady Liberty*. Clearly visible in the lefthand pilot seat is 1st Lt. Ralph R. Miller, the pilot. Although the official caption states that the picture was taken just seconds before *Lady Liberty* was hit by flak over Flushing, it is obvious that, in fact, it was taken during group assembly, as the airfield which is visible on the ground, is Chelveston, home of the 305th Bomb Group. USAAF

alarm-bell, I couldn't move; the wheel and stick were pushing against me and the speed on the dive had me pasted to the seat like the paper on the wall. Five, six, seven seconds sitting there, helplessly watching the ground come up. What a shock to realize that you had just "had it", not just watching someone else as it had been before. What a ghastly, sickening feeling to have time to realize that you would be dead in a few seconds. Then all thoughts stopped.

I opened my eyes with the sudden realization that I was alive, I couldn't believe it, I had a vivid picture on those last frightening seconds. I took time for the peaceful quiet to impress me and I realized I was in a car with two *Luftwaffe* guards, an officer and a driver. My wet clothes, open parachute and half inflated life preserver were under my feet. I was dressed in a strange type fatigue suit and had heavy bandages on my head. I began to feel the severe cuts there. My left ankle was sprained and there were wounds on my legs. "What happened, how am I alive, where is the rest of the crew?" It was to be a long time before I had the answers to all of these questions.

Only one other of Miller's crew miraculously survived. This was tail gunner Staff Sgt. Emil Radosevich, who bailed out his own escape hatch during the fall of the tail assembly to the ground. It is highly probable that the parachutes which were observed by Wing Cmdr. Johnnie Johnson south of Flushing were those of Ralph Miller and Emil Radosevich.

After a direct hit by one of the shells fired by *Marine-Flak-Abteilung 810, Lady Liberty* has broken up. The forward half of the bomber and several smaller parts fall toward the Westerscheldt. Only pilot Ralph Miller and tail gunner Emil Radosevich survived the tragedy. On the South Beveland peninsula, the village of Borssele can just be discerned. USAAF

A few seconds later: *Lady Liberty* going down toward the Westerscheldt. At the far right-hand side of the picture, the old Dutch fort of Rammekens can be discerned. USAAF

The bodies of six crewmembers of *Lady Liberty* washed ashore in the weeks following the mission: left waist gunner Sgt. Wiliam J. Crouch and engineer Tech Sgt. Bynum C. Crabtree on August 20, navigator 2nd Lt. Donald J. McGowan on August 26, copilot 2nd Lt. John F. Meade on August 28, bombardier 2nd Lt. Joseph M. McGinley on August 31, and finally radio operator Tech Sgt. Fulton F. Horn on September 1. All six were buried in the Northern Cemetery in Flushing. After the war, they were temporarily reinterred at the American Military Cemetery Ardennes, near Neuville-en-Condroz in Belgium. McGinley and Crouch still have their final resting place there; the four others were repatriated to the United States and are permanently interred in cemeteries in Massachusetts, New Jersey, Texas, and North Carolina.

Staff Sgt. Edgar G. Lott, posing at his battle station, the right waist gun of *Lady Liberty*. He is still missing in action. DEBBIE MILLER HUGHES

Two crewmembers are still missing in action until the present day. They are ball-turret gunner Staff Sgt. Albert F. Miller Jr. and right waist gunner Staff Sgt. Edgar G. Lott. Their names are inscribed on the walls of the missing at the American Military Cemetery in Margraten, the Netherlands.

Over the Flushing harbor, with clear evidence of earlier bombing attacks, the bombs of the 305th Bomb Group are released, as witnessed by the camera aboard B-17F 42-29870, flown by 2nd Lt. L. R. Hart. On the second frame, falling bombs are visible over the middle of the airfield, and on the third frame, another series of bombs starts to explode in the northeast corner of the field. USAAF

Many crewmembers in the 305th Bomb Group had seen with awe what had happened to *Lady Liberty* and her crew. Perhaps the lead bombardier was also distracted by this gruesome sight, as immediately after the flak hit, things went wrong aboard *Lallah-V III*, the lead ship of the 102nd Combat Wing.

A small mistake with his complicated Norden bomb sight resulted in the salvo of only two out of sixteen of Lieutenant Metcalf's bombs. After a delay of approximately ten seconds past the bomb-release line, he toggled the rest of his bombs out. This resulted in all of the lead and low squadrons' bombs falling over. The high squadron leader had dropped on his own range and these bombs fell to the right of the aiming point, but just on the northern edge of the airfield. In all, the 305th Bomb Group had dropped 288 300-pound M-31 general-purpose bombs.

The 306th Bomb Group fared no better. Lead bombardier 1st Lt. W. Z. Morey reported that because of the short bomb run, he had too little time to make the final adjustments in his Norden bombsight. The 320 M-31 bombs of the twenty B-17F's in this group now also fell to the right of the aiming point, outside the airfield.

This left the 92nd Bomb Group as only group still to bomb Flushing airfield. This group's lead bombardier, Lt. J. Ryan, also reported the bomb run being too short for accurate adjustments in his Norden sight. It is apparent that the wind velocity on the cross-wind bomb run caused most of the bombs of the three groups in the 102nd Combat Wing to fall to the right of the target. All 272 M-31 bombs of the 92nd Bomb Group fell northeast of the field, along the canal about 500 to 1,000 yards away from the target.

This time the Germans reported only minor damage to the airfield, with four soldiers killed on and around it. The Dutch population living in the vicinity of the airfield suffered heavier. Fourteen civilians were killed by the bombs of the three groups, according to reports of the Civil Air Defense. Four days before, forty-one civilians had been killed in Flushing; now the casualties fell in the hamlets of East and West Souburg.[*]

Sara Diermanse from East Souburg, then seventeen years old, recalls:

> My sister had recently given birth to a baby girl, Sara. Her husband was imprisoned by the Germans, somewhere in the vicinity of Berlin. My brother Willem had that evening gone over to our sister's house to help her out in some way. I usually spent a lot of time there, too.

[*]The names of all civilian fatal casualties are recorded in Appendix A.

The camera aboard 1st Lt. Winston J. Tucker's B-17F 42-30408 recorded the moment of release of the bombs of the 92nd Bomb Group and these hitting in and around the canal through Walcheren. At the lefthand bottom of the first picture, Rammekens is plainly visible; in the top lefthand corner is the village East-Souburg. In the second picture, on the lefthand bottom is East-Souburg. On the other side of the canal, West-Souburg, the airfield, and the bomb bursts of the 305th Bomb Group. At the far right is the city of Middelburg. USAAF

Flushing under the bombs, as seen from 21,000 feet. On the left is Flushing with its airfield and harbor; on the right is Middelburg. At the bottom of the picture is the old Dutch fort of Rammekens. The hits were analyzed by intelligence officers and were described as follows: A shows at least thirty bursts in and near the dispersal area in the northeast corner of the airfield, while A1 shows at least seven bursts in a bomb storage area. B shows at least sixty-six bursts in fields from half a mile to one and a half miles northwest of the target area. Both A and B can be attributed to the 305th Bomb Group. C shows at least twenty-three bursts in fields approximately two miles east of the target area. D shows at least twenty-nine bursts in fields approximately two miles northeast of the target area. C and D are results of the bombs of the 306th Bomb Group. This picture does not show the more than 120 bombs from the 92nd Bomb Group that would straddle the canal about one and a half miles from the target area, between A and D, a few seconds after this picture was taken. From the location of *Marine-Flak-Batterie West* on the Nolledike (in line with the rear of the arrow), smoke drifts over the Westerscheldt—proof of its continuous fire on the bomber formations. PUBLIC RECORD OFFICE

Then the bombers came and the bombs fell. We immediately tried to go over to their place, but were stopped on the road. At first, somebody told me that everything was OK. But then we learned that my brother and the baby were killed. My sister was slightly injured and was treated at the spot. After we were allowed to go to the houses, we tried to salvage as much property as we could. It was such a sad thing to do.

After the bombs were dropped, the three groups took up a proper combat wing formation again and headed for their bases. No German fighters had been encountered because of the very effective escort by the Royal Air Force.

After an uneventful return flight, the 305th Bomb Group landed between 1900 and 1916 hours on Chelveston, the 92nd Bomb Group reached Alconbury at 1902 hours, and finally the 306th Bomb Group arrived at 1913 at Thurleigh.

Below, and on the following pages:
Grim results of the bombs which missed Flushing airfield. M. SANDERSE

CHAPTER 5

Gilze-Rijen

As explained earlier, for this mission, the 103rd Combat Wing was by necessity a composite wing, comprising groups of both the 101st and 103rd Combat Wings. Because of heavy losses on the mission to Schweinfurt two days earlier, several bomb groups were unable to provide more than a single squadron's strength of planes on the nineteenth. The 381st Bomb Group for example had lost no less than eleven of its B-17s over Schweinfurt, the 91st Bomb Group lost ten Fortresses with their crews. Morale was at low ebb on Ridgewell and Bassingbourn. The crews lost had made up a large proportion of the available experienced combat crews of the groups concerned, and these were now left with a large number of comparatively new crews. Everett Malone, an original copilot in the 381st Bomb Group, recalls: "Within the first ninety days overseas, only seven officers remained in the 535rd Bomb Squadron, out of the original thirty-five. Our morale was very low—this job had no future."

For the mission to Gilze-Rijen, the wing was to be led by a composite group, comprising a lead squadron of the 384th Bomb Group from Grafton Underwood and high and low squadrons of the 379th Bomb Group from Kimbolton. The combat wing commander was to be the commanding officer of the 384th Bomb Group, Col. Budd J. Peaslee. Peaslee himself had flown on the Schweinfurt mission and lost five B-17s and their crews from his command.

The high group of the wing was also a composite group. Its lead squadron was provided by the 91st Bomb Group from Bassingbourn, the high squadron by the 351st Bomb Group from Polebrook and the low squadron by the 381st Bomb Group from Ridgewell. These three groups had lost no fewer than twenty-three B-17s among them on the Schweinfurt mission. Leading this composite group were Maj. John C. Bishop and Capt. Harry T. Lay in B-17F 42-29921 *Oklahoma Okie*. Lay had flown on the Schweinfurt mission as well. The radio operator of his crew was killed during the fighter attacks that day.

The low group was a standard formation; all ships and crews were provided by the 303rd Bomb Group from Molesworth. This unit had lost no

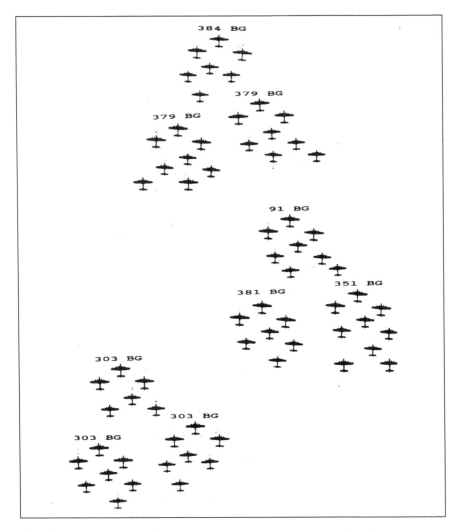

The planned combat wing formation: three groups, each comprising three squadrons, that were furnished by the bomb groups as noted above them.

ships on the mission to Schweinfurt and thus was able to put up a complete group formation, which was led by Maj. William R. Calhoun, Jr., and Capt. Glynn F. Shumake in B-17F 41-24635 *The 8 Ball Mk II*. As the assembly of the 103rd Composite Combat Wing was to be very chaotic, finally leading to *ad hoc* leadership and even inaccurate bombing of this wing, and therefore was to have a profound effect on the outcome of the mission, it is worth studying in great detail.

In view of things to come, it is difficult to understand why the composite group of Col. Budd Peaslee was assigned to lead the wing in the first place. Even an ordinary group assembly was no easy undertaking in itself. Assembling a composite group out of three squadrons from two different bomb groups was, of course, even more difficult. Then to burden this composite group also with leading the wing was asking for trouble. We will see what happened.

A supplement to Field Order 182, which all bomb groups had received by teletype, not only gave the composition of the 103rd Combat Wing, as explained above, but also gave the following instructions and details for its assembly. They give a clear insight in the complicated task of assembling a combat wing.

—The group commander of 384 Group will be combat wing commander.

—103 Combat Wing will assemble on line Molesworth to Peterborough.

—384 Bomb Group will arrange for the assembly of the composite group and will also furnish deputy group leader.

—Lead group will depart Molesworth at zero-hour minus 40 minutes at 6,000 feet or 2,000 feet above low clouds.

—Route after assembly: Peterborough to King's Lynn to Ipswich to Orfordness. Begin climb at Peterborough.

—Time schedule:

Molesworth	Z - 40 minutes at 6,000 feet
Peterborough	Z - 35 minutes
King's Lynn	Z - 25 minutes
Ipswich	Z - 5 minutes
Orfordness	Z-hour at 20,000 feet

—Group furnished by 101 Combat Wing will fire red-red flares at combat wing assembly. Lead group (composite) will fire green-green followed by yellow-red.

—303 Bomb Group will fire green-green flares followed by green-red.

Colonel Budd J. Peaslee, the designated wing leader, later submitted a report about the episode that followed:

The lead squadron of the 103rd Combat Wing, consisting of seven airplanes from this group, took off from Ridgewell at 1600 hours and proceeded to assemble over the field. We left the base at 1616 hours and continued to climb in the direction of Kimbolton. The briefed assembly at Kimbolton was to be at 6,000 feet, however, it was necessary to climb through the broken clouds to 8,000 feet. At Kimbolton, the squadron proceeded to circle and called the 379th Bomb Group on VHF advising them that assembly would be on top of the cloud layer. No acknowledgement was received. After some time had elapsed, a formation of thirteen airplanes was observed below the overcast. Flares were fired; however, it is not known whether they were seen or not as the formation was ahead of us. Eventually, at about departure time from Molesworth, another formation of thirteen airplanes was observed, on top of the overcast, and it was assumed that this was the remainder of the composite group. Flares were fired, no acknowledgement was received, no answers were given. A group was seen at about this time which was approaching head-on and flares were again dropped, identifying our organization and again, no answer was received. However, this group started a 180-degree turn and it was assumed that they intended to join. Now, at departure time, there were three formations visible; one of thirteen airplanes, a complete group and our own. My squadron proceeded on course with what is believed to have been the remainder approximately three miles off to the left and the complete group in trail. On the next leg, the group in the rear turned short and the formation of thirteen airplanes finally turned in trail a considerable distance behind. A 360-degree turn was performed at Peterborough in an attempt to get the combat wing together.

Reading between the lines of this official report, we can feel the despair mount aboard the lead ship. How agonizing the search for the 379th Bomb Group planes must have been for Colonel Peaslee. He was not only responsible for getting his own composite group together, but also for the subsequent assembly of the combat wing, three group formations in all. The responsibility for a combat leader was a heavy burden.

Now let us see how both squadrons of the 379th Bomb Group fared. They were the ones that Peaslee was so desperately looking for. We will first

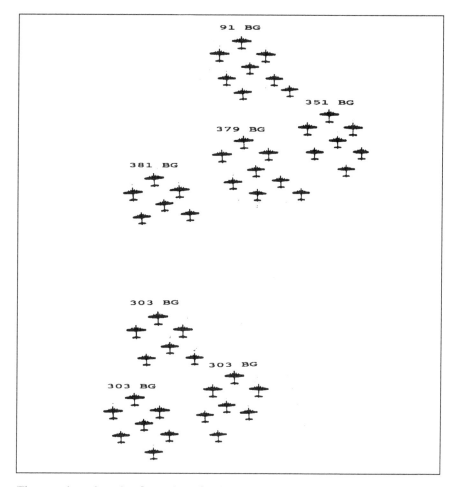

The actual combat wing formation after its assembly. The lead and high groups have merged and made up a nonstandard four-squadron group. Several aircraft have returned with mechanical failures. The low group has assembled as planned.

take up the report submitted by Lt. Noble M. Johnson, who was leading the low squadron in B-17F 42-29963 *Judy*.

> We took off from Kimbolton on time and assembled over the field at 1,500 feet. We started to climb to 6,000 feet. The clouds at 6,000 feet extended to about 7,000 feet. We climbed 2,000 feet above to 9,000 feet and made one circle of the field and at 1620 hours a nine-ship formation approached to the east, to our left. They made

a turn to the left and we tried to tack onto them in that turn. Before we could tack on, they made another turn, to the right and they were about ten minutes from the field before we ever got into position. It was then that we could see the "J" on their tails [B-17s of the 351st Bomb Group]. We knew then that it was the wrong squadron, but as we were going in our approximate course, we stayed with them, trying to find the planes of the 384th Bomb Group.

From Peterborough, they headed southeast and started to climb. We still had not seen the 384th and tried to call them on VHF, but could get no reply, but we did hear Brownlow of the high squadron. He also was calling the 384th to ask them to fire a flare. We still heard no reply from the 384th or anyone else or did we see any flares. From then on, we flew with them in the low squadron position and they took a position leading the high group.

Lieutenant William G. Brownlow III, leading the designated high squadron for the composite group in B-17F 42-30237 *Stump Jumper*, reported:

Took off and formed as the high squadron over Lieutenant Johnson's squadron. Circled the field and climbed up above the clouds. A nine ship formation came over the field. We fired flares and got no reply. Lieutenant Johnson formed on them as low squadron. We therefore followed suit and formed as high squadron. Markings of lead squadron were "J". We again fired flares and got no reply. We fired flares to identify 379th Group. I tried to contact both the lead squadron and Lieutenant Johnson on VHF, with no results. We continued circling and flew into the area of Peterborough. We saw two separate squadrons approaching individually and fired flares, but did not see flares from these squadrons. At the time we should have passed on course we headed for the coast as a Group. At the coast, another squadron, with "A" identification [91st Bomb Group], approached and the formation arrived at was "A" lead, "J" high, and Lieutenant Johnson low. This was an eighteen-ship formation. There was an twenty-one ship formation flying low group. There were no other planes but ours. Upon seeing that we were now alone in the high group, I determined to bring the squadron back.

Then let us quote from the report that Capt. Robert H. Johnson made up. Johnson was leading the planes of the 351st Bomb Group (the "J" squadron mentioned in the accounts), flying in B-17F 42-29812 *Lucifer Jr.*

We took off on schedule, climbing to 10,000 feet over the field and proceeded toward Bassingbourn. In attempting to locate our composite
group, we flew near a lead and low squadron, who immediately tacked
on to us, forming a group. We next went to Peterborough, where the
high squadron left us, and we turned to a collision heading to our composite group. We joined them and with an odd low squadron tacked on
to us, we climbed 500 feet per minute to 21,000 feet.

Now back to unlucky Col. Budd J. Peaslee, the combat wing leader, still
searching fruitlessly for his own low and high squadrons. These, as we have
just read, had erroneously tacked onto the 351st Bomb Group's squadron.
Then, if Peaslee would have been able to find his missing squadrons, he still
had to assemble his combat wing into a proper formation.

Prior to the arrival at the point of departure on the English coast, a
message was sent to First Bombardment Wing stating the formation
would make good the mission fifteen minutes late. This was acknowledged and at the point of departure a slow 360-degree turn was
made in order to allow the wing to assemble. This was not accomplished because the units proceeded on out to sea approximately ten
miles south of the point of departure. This threw our lead squadron
far behind and we would have never been able to catch the other
formations. At this point, it was realized that it would be futile to
continue attempts to assemble the wing and a message was sent by
VHF instructing the participating units of the 103rd Combat Wing to
return to bases. This was not acknowledged. An additional message
was sent to the First Bombardment Wing stating that the formation
was returning to base. VHF was checked with one of the other airplanes in the squadron and he reported reception loud and clear.
Upon return to the base, it was necessary to circle approximately
twenty minutes to enable the bombardiers to safety the bombs. Two
aircraft could not safety bombs and were dispatched to The Wash
with instructions to salvo them in The Wash.

The assembly of the 103rd Composite Combat Wing had thus been a
total failure. Instead of three groups, each comprising three squadrons, now
two groups, one of four squadrons (one each of the 91st, 351st, 381st, and
379th Bomb Groups) and one of three squadrons (all of the 303rd Bomb
Group), proceeded to the enemy coast. Two squadrons, one each of the
379th and 384th Bomb Groups, had returned to Kimbolton and Grafton
Underwood, respectively.

B-17F 42-29921 *Oklahoma Okie* of the 91st Bomb Group, 324th Bomb Squadron. This B-17 led all American bombers on the Schweinfurt mission of August 17. Flown by Maj. John Bishop and Capt. Harry Lay, it ended up leading the composite combat wing toward Gilze-Rijen airfield on August 19. *Oklahoma Okie* was lost on December 31, 1943, on a mission to Bordeaux, France. USAAF

The men now leading the combat wing, instead of just their composite high group as assigned, were Maj. John C. Bishop and Capt. Harry T. Lay in *Oklahoma Okie* of the 91st Bomb Group. At first, they had no problems in assembling their own formation. Lay's narrative does clearly illustrate the confusion that developed over the North Sea, when nobody knew where the assigned wing leader, Colonel Peaslee, was.

The 91st Bomb Group took off and assembled eight ships at 2,000 feet, climbed to 9,500 feet, which was 2,000 feet above clouds, and assembled with the 381st formation and left base on time. Flew flight plan, and were at prescribed altitude at King's Lynn from which point flight plan was carried out and we left the coast at Orfordness about a half minute late, picking up squadron from 351st completing our composite formation.

Could see group coming up on our right from King's Lynn to coast and they joined us there as high group. We thought they were lead group and tried to get on top of them, but they climbed also, so we had to take over the lead. At the coast, tail gunner reported low group coming up from behind and they assembled as our low group about mid-Channel.

Most of *Oklahoma Okie*'s crew on August 19 were pictured in late May 1943 on Bassingbourn. Kneeling from left to right: 2nd Lt. Roger W. Fuller (bombardier, flew with Flight Officer Pitts), 2nd Lt. William F. Campbell (navigator, flew with Lieutenant Arp aboard *Bomb-Boogie*), and 1st Lt. Harry T. Lay (pilot). Standing from left to right: Staff Sgt. Vernon O. Miller (right waist gunner), Staff Sgt. William A. Gottschalk (ball turret gunner), Staff Sgt. Clarence W. Clark (tail gunner), Tech Sgt. Donald F. Robertson (radio operator, killed in action on August 17), Tech Sgt. Roy C. Cameron (engineer), and Staff Sgt. Louie R. Rivera (left waist gunner, not on mission). USAAF

Where the reports now speak about a combat wing, it is apparent that no really good defensive formation was established. It was more a column of four individual squadrons and one group formation making their way to Gilze-Rijen.

Three crews in the 103rd Composite Combat Wing aborted the mission due to mechnical failure of their aircraft. B-17F 42-29861 *Buck-Shot* of the 351st Bomb Group was returned because of an oil leak in number-three engine. B-17F 42-3152 *Sleepy Lagoon* of the same group had its number one engine running rough, investigation later revealed a broken valve. *Buck Shot* brought its twenty 100-pound bombs back to Polebrook; those of *Sleepy Lagoon* were jettisoned over the North Sea. Finally, B-17F 42-29755 *Last Straw* of the 381st Bomb Group returned with a blown supercharger on one of its engines and brought its bombs back to Ridgewell.

A good account of the flight of the depleted combat wing over the North Sea is given by Capt. David S. Clifton, who was leading the high squadron of the 303rd Bomb Group, in B-17F 42-5434 *Lady Luck*:

> We proceeded from base on course alone toward Peterborough. The other two groups failed to rendezvous with us although we were at 5,000 feet. We climbed through overcast near Peterborough and fell in behind a group and fired flares. This group appeared to be a whole group plus a separate squadron, both having poor formation. The 303rd Bomb Group was in good formation. We departed coast trailing this group at a very large interval and about mid-Channel a high group of about fourteen aircraft pulled up in view directly above us. This group held its position for about three minutes, then turned back to the left and left us heading back for England. We leveled off at 19,000 feet, still about a mile behind the lead group, which was at about 21,000 feet and one squadron flying high position on them. We attempted to pull up onto them before reaching the enemy coast, by indicating 170 miles per hour. They made one "S"-turn just before reaching the coast, evidently to allow us to catch up, but we followed in trail failing to close in on them. We never closed up into a supporting defensive formation. There was at least a thousand feet between the highest aircraft in the 303rd and the lowest aircraft in their group and we were trailing about half a mile.

In this rather unorganized situation, the groups entered the airspace over German-occupied Holland, made rendezvous with the friendly fighters, and took up their heading for Gilze-Rijen. As described earlier, their fighter escort was provided by the 56th and 353rd Fighter Groups, which made rendezvous between 1747 and 1750 hours over the Dutch coast.

The bomber formation was now nearing its assigned initial point, near Bergen op Zoom. A few flak bursts were observed, but the flak up to this point was generally reported as being "meager, but fairly accurate." However, no ships were lost or critically damaged at this stage of the attack.

For a clearer picture of the ensuing events of the combat wing, the rest of this chapter is split up. First, we will look at the exploits of the American fighter escort. Then we will focus on the four squadrons in the lead group, their bombing, their encounters with German fighters, and their return to England. Finally, this same procedure will be followed for the 303rd Bomb Group, which was trailing the lead group. Although this way of dealing with

P-47s of the 78th Fighter Group are ready for take-off from Duxford.
HAROLD P. BAHNEMANN

the events is not strictly chronological, narrative cohesion is better pre-
served this way.

This is also the best moment to discuss briefly the validity of victory
claims in combat. The air war was a struggle of life and death. Both personal
victory and that of the 8th Air Force in general was measured in enemies
shot down and compared with own losses. The loss of sixty B-17s on August
17 on the Schweinfurt/Regensburg mission didn't look too bad in the headlines of the papers, compared with the 307 German fighters that were
claimed destroyed by the Americans. However, actual German losses that
day did not exceed thirty.

Especially for fighter pilots, the coveted status of "ace," for five enemies
destroyed, was the ultimate goal. The gunners aboard the American
bombers eagerly counted their victories as well, and they present also the
most obvious examples of exaggerated claims. Sometimes, dozens of gunners in a formation were firing on only one or two incoming German fighters. If one of these was seen to go down, often more than one gunner
submitted a claim for its destruction. Although a claim had to be substanti-
ated by at least one other crewmember and an official victory credit board at
wing headquarters scrutinized all claims coming in from the various bomb
groups, it is obvious that far more German fighters were awarded as
"destroyed" than the actual losses could justify. However, probably in order

to keep morale high, a liberal attitude toward the award of fighters destroyed or damaged was maintained. But also the fighter pilots exagerated. Here again, actual losses do not match with the awarded claims for fighters destroyed. Although most of the combat reports contain the phrases "seen to explode," "saw it hit the ground," or "saw the pilot bail out," it is obvious that this could not always have been backed up by facts. Gun-camera film was used for the evaluation of the claims of the fighter pilots, so they are more valid than those of the bomber gunners, but exaggerated they are.

However, it was not only the Americans who were at fault. German claims were also too high. The story for the German fighter pilots is similar to that of their American counterparts above. But even the German flak claimed too many victims. For example, in the previous chapter, we saw how the flak unit that destroyed *Lady Liberty* of the 305th Bomb Group claimed another B-17 and a fighter shot down in the same engagement. Needless to say, this was not backed up by the facts. The reader should keep this in mind while reading the following chapters.

The escort for the combat wing heading for Gilze-Rijen was provided by the 56th Fighter Group from Halesworth, comprising the 61st, 62nd, and 63rd Fighter Squadrons, and the 353rd Fighter Group from Metfield, comprising the 350th, 351st, and 352nd Fighter Squadrons.

The fifty-one P-47 Thunderbolts of the experienced 56th Fighter Group were led by the group commanding officer, Col. Hubert A. Zemke. They took off from Halesworth at 1717 hours. Two fighter pilots aborted, and the forty-nine remaining made landfall between Schouwen and Walcheren Island at 1747 hours, at 25,000 feet. Rendezvous with the B-17s, their "big friends," was made just east of Woensdrecht at 27,000 feet.

The forty-two Thunderbolts of the 353rd Fighter Group were led by their brand-new commanding officer, Maj. Loren G. McCollum. McCollum had only just taken over command of the group, after his predecessor, Lt. Col. Joseph A. Morris, had gone down over Paris on the mission of August 16. The 353rd Fighter Group had also only recently become operational, it flew its first mission on August 9. After three fighter sweeps and four previous escorts, this was only their fifth escort mission for the bombers. After taking off from Metfield at 1701 hours, seven of the forty-two fighter pilots returned for various reasons. Those remaining crossed the Dutch coast at Haamstede at 1746 hours, at 25,500 feet and made rendezvous with the bombers at the western tip of Tholen Island at 1750 hours.

The bomber formations were at this time approaching their assigned Initial Point, near Bergen op Zoom. The German fighter controller (Jagdführer Holland/Ruhr) had been able to assemble about 130 of his fighters over southern Holland. They came from airfields such as Schiphol, Woensdrecht, Venlo, Bergen, Deelen, and Mönchengladbach.

A typical *Gruppe* take-off on July 25, 1943. *Hauptmann* Klaus Mietusch leads his III./JG 26 into battle from Nordholz. WERNER MÖSZNER

The first encounters between the opposing fighter pilots were in the vicinity of Breda, shortly after 1800 hours. The 56th Fighter Group was in the thick of the battle.

Capt. Gerald W. Johnson was leading its Keyworth Blue Flight in his P-47D 42-7877 *In the Mood*. He reported:

> As we neared the first bomber formation, I saw three unidentified planes flying parallel and on our left in the opposite direction at our altitude, 25,000 feet. They made a large turn to the left and started in on our tail and at this point were about 2,000 feet below us. I watched them come in and when they were about 1,000 yards behind us I called a break to the left. We made a tight 360-degree turn and came out on their tail. They were Me 109s flying line abreast. As we made this turn they continued flying straight with the exception that the leader did a very quick slow roll and then continued straight. I fired about a one second burst from about 250 yards at 15 degrees deflection at the number three plane. I saw strikes on the wing near the fuselage. He immediately flipped over and went straight down. I let him go and pulled up in a tight left turn and found the leader of these three straight in front of me at about 100 yards. I started firing and he tried all kinds of maneuvres, with the exception of breaking down as they ordinarily do. I could see flashes on his fuselage and knew I was hitting him. Pretty soon, there was a large red flash near the centre of the fuselage and he started down in a rather steep dive, trailing smoke. I watched him go down for about 10,000 feet and then pulled up to try to get my flight together again. Lieutenant Biales, who was flying in the second flight in our section saw him hit the ground. Our flight was broken up so badly by these attacks that we couldn't rejoin, so I joined Keyworth White flight and completed the mission without further incident.
>
> I claim one Me 109 destroyed and one Me 109 damaged, at 1802 hours near Gilze-Rijen.

By destroying this Me 109 with 486 rounds of his .50 caliber, Gerald W. Johnson had raised his score to four-and-a-half confirmed air victories.[*]

---

[*] Some books state that with this victory, Johnson became the first ace of the 56th Fighter Group. However, since his victory on August 17 was split with Frank McCauley, this is not true. Zemke became the group's first ace on October 2. Johnson was made prisoner of war on March 27, 1944, after being shot down by flak while strafing a road convoy. By then, he was a major, commanded the 63rd Fighter Squadron, and had obtained no fewer than eighteen confirmed air victories.

Flying as Keyworth Blue 2—Gerald Johnson's wing man—was 1st Lt Robert S. Johnson in his P-47C 41-6253:

We were a little bit east and north of Woensdrecht when four Me 109s came in at us from the same level, about 25,000 feet, from about five o'clock. We had not quite reached the bombers. My leader turned left and pulled it slightly up. We made a 360-degree turn and came in at the Me 109s from about seven o'clock to them. They had not turned from their original track, evidently thinking we were scared completely off. When they saw us coming in they rolled over and went in different directions but kept their altitude. One, the leader, pulled to the left and started climbing. Captain Johnson, my leader, had begun to turn left after him. I followed slightly below my leader and not twenty-five yards behind him. Captain Johnson let a burst go and the Me 109 immediately broke right and spun. I was in good position then and fired at him in the slow spin. I saw strikes and smoke began to come from him. He pulled out of the spin and started straight down. Captain Johnson had pulled up and I thought he was watching my tail, so I rolled over and going straight down on his tail I opened up again. Strikes were seen all over him and very much more smoke poured out. I tried to pull out as he went slightly to the left in a steep dive. I was gaining speed rapidly and my ship shuddered all over. As I finally pulled it out at 12,000 to 15,000 feet, I saw the pilot, also being in a very shallow dive, roll on his side and a chute opened. The Me 109 then plowed into the ground and I returned to the P-47s above the bombers. I claim one Me 109 destroyed, at 1802 hours northeast of Woensdrecht.

This combat report clearly shows the eager and aggressive attitude of this fighter pilot. Destroying this Me 109 with only 278 rounds from his .50 caliber, Johnson obtained his second confirmed air victory. Robert S. Johnson would soon rise to great fame. He ended his fighting days in May 1944 when he returned to the United States, with twenty-seven destroyed enemy fighters to his credit, as the third ranking fighter ace in the European theater of operations.

First Lieutenant Frank E. McCauley was flying in P-47C 41-6271 *Rat Racer* as number 3 in Keyworth Red Flight and also became engaged:

We had made landfall and were about ten miles west of Gilze-Rijen at 27,000 feet when at least one Me 109 came at us from seven o'clock and slightly above. Our flight leader broke hard left. When

I was at ninety degree to him, I saw him fire a burst. He must have been firing at my wing man, Lieutenant Barnum, for he was trailing me and the Me 109 did have nearly enough deflection for my ship. He fired at about 400 yards. I lost sight of him.

In breaking, I lost the rest of the flight, but was able to pick up Keyworth Red 2, Lieutenant Powers, who flew the rest of the mission as my wing man. We were over the bombers in the vicinity of Oosterhout when we saw three Me 109s in front of and slightly above the bombers. I dove down at one of them and he started to make a climbing turn into me. When he was at about 200 yards from me and about ten to twenty degrees from head on, I fired a burst and kept on leading him and firing until he was under me. That was at 18,000 feet. Lieutenant Powers observed the plane burst into flames and go into a spin and crash.

We pulled up and flew over the bombers for a while at about 22,000 feet. Near Schoonhoven we saw a flight of four Me 109s in string formation at about 18,000 feet start to go in on the rear of the bombers. We did a half roll and went down to attack. I ended up astern of the rear Me 109 about 300 yards back. I closed to about 200 yards and fired a burst. I could see hits and smoke coming from the engine. I tried to slow up so I could make sure of the plane being destroyed but was rapidly closing. I fired one or two more bursts before I had to pull up to avoid collision. The plane went into a steep spiral, still emitting smoke and finally crashed in a mass of flames. Meanwhile, the other three Me 109s broke for the deck.

We climbed back up from 12,000 feet, where the last combat took place and headed out. We were about the same level as the bombers, when I saw one bomber leave the formation over Rotterdam. He was immediately attacked by enemy aircraft and also encountered flak. We tried but were unable to gain enough altitude to cross over the top of the bombers to help him.

Lieutenant Powers did a very thorough job in covering me. The full cooperation of a wing man has proven invaluable in combat.

McCauley had used only 729 rounds of .50 caliber for the destruction of the two Me 109s, which was confirmed by his gun-camera film. He ended his flying career as an ace, with six confirmed air victories. In his account, he mentioned that an Me 109 apparently shot at his wingman, 1st Lt. Eugene E. Barnum. He was right. According to Barnum, "I was flying at 25,000 feet. As we broke, an Me 109 was coming in on my tail fast. He opened fire shortly after our break and continued to shoot till he had passed my tail."

This battle damage to the engine of Eugene Barnum's P-47C 41-6337 was caused by
German bullets on August 19. USAAF

Upon Barnum's return to Halesworth, it was found that his P-47C 41-6337 had been hit by one small-caliber bullet, which caused damage to the oil tank and oxygen regulator.

First Lieutenant Michael J. Quirk of the 62nd Fighter Squadron was flying in P-47C 41-6215:

> I was leading the second element of Red Flight and we were just approaching the bombers north-east of Woensdrecht when we were attacked from the rear by three FW 190s. The whole flight broke left and after pulling up and circling around a few times I discovered that Red Four and myself had lost the first element, so we flew over to the B-17s and tacked on to another flight of P-47s. After covering the 17s for a while, we started home, and about ten miles from the bombers, I saw two FW 190s flying southwest at about 19,000 feet. Red 4 and I dove on them from 27,000 feet, and they broke in different directions, so I took the number two ship. He broke left and then, instead of completing his turn, started to break right, giving me a beautiful set-up for a dead astern attack. I opened fire first at about 600 yards—waited—then fired again at about 350 yards and closed to 200. I could see strikes all over the cockpit and engine, large pieces flew off and the ship burst into flames. He suddenly rolled over on his back as I pulled up and I lost him then, but Lieutenant Adrianse (63rd Squadron), who was preparing to attack him, saw him explode in mid-air, as well as Captain Dauphin (62nd Squadron). After pulling up, Red 4 and I joined Lieutenant Adrianse and another P-47 and came home.

With 582 rounds of .50 caliber, Quirk had attained the first of his eleven confirmed air victories.

Not all American fighter pilots of the 56th Fighter Group were able to provide fighter cover for the bombers. First Lieutenant Glenn L. Hodges of the 63rd Fighter Squadron was piloting P-47C 41-6216, with fuselage code UN-W. His plane suffered from engine trouble, a drop in the manifold pressure, and was escorted home by one of his flight members, 1st Lt. Harold E. Comstock, in P-47C 41-6326. Comstock tells what happened:

> About 1804 hours. Lieutenant Hodges, who was Postgate Red 4, called and said that his engine was cutting out and that he was going back. I told him to go ahead and that I would cover him. This was approximately over Breda at 27,000 feet.

Glenn L. Hodges of the 56th Fighter Group, who ditched his P-47C 41-6216 near Hellevoetsluis and was made prisoner of war.
JOHN H. TRULUCK JR.

Hodges started to lose altitude and continued to do so at a gliding speed of 180 miles per hour until we were over Tholen Island. He then nosed it down and was doing about 220 to 230 miles per hour when we crossed the coast line of Tholen Island and were out in the middle of Oosterscheldt estuary. He was right on the deck and I was around 200 feet above him and behind. He continued to lose speed until he was stalling and he ditched. His nose went up and then settled back. Needless to say, the flak had been shooting at us ever since we were at 1,000 feet.

There were quite a number of grey coloured boats that I thought might be Dutch fishing boats so I didn't fire at them. They were not fishing boats but were flak boats or rescue launches as I soon found out. There were fifteen or sixteen lined up on either side of the channel so I gave a short burst at them and continued my violent evasive action. Never touched me.

When I last saw Lieutenant Hodges, he was in his plane which was landing in the Oosterscheldt estuary north of North-Beveland Island at about 1810 hours.

Harold E. Comstock posing on Halesworth with his P-47C 41-6326, coded UN-Y.
He also flew this ship on August 19, when he tried to escort Hodges home. The
swastika denoted Comstock's first air victory, an Me 109 that he shot down on the
August 17 mission, escorting the bombers returning from Schweinfurt. Having run
out of fuel, Comstock crash-landed this P-47 on February 3, 1944, on Halesworth.
HAROLD E. COMSTOCK

Hodges had actually ditched in the Haringvliet near Hellevoetsluis. He
clambered out of the cockpit and jumped in the water, inflating his life preserver, or Mae West. He was quickly picked up alive and well by the Germans
and had to spend the remainder of the war in Stalag Luft III.

By now, the fighting gradually moved toward the Dutch coastline, the
American fighters had used almost all of the time they could spend in the
target area. Because of their limited fuel capacity, it was time to get back to
England. However, the dogfights continued.

First Lieutenant Joseph L. Egan Jr. of the 63rd Fighter Squadron was flying in his P-47C 41-6584. His combat report follows:

I was flying in Postgate Blue Flight (Captain Burke, Lieutenant Peppers, Lieutenant Egan, Lieutenant Batdorf) as number 3. We had
joined the bombers near the target and they were circling around
them at about 27,000 feet trying to find a target to attack. Captain

Burke, the leader of Blue Flight, had made one pass at two FW 190s and another at two Messerschmitt 210s, but had to discontinue with attacks because of evasive action taken by the enemy.

Just after these passes, about 1817 hours, my wingman, Lieutenant Batdorf who I had lost sight of by this time, called me saying that he was going home with three other P-47s because of a shortage of fuel. At this point, about 1820 hours, Captain Burke made a ninety-degree turn left and took a heading of approximately west. I swung to the outside of this turn to avoid passing him, and as I did so, I noticed two FW 190s about 4,000 feet below also heading west in the direction of the bombers. I called Captain Burke and told him that I was going to get myself a 190. In order to get behind the Huns, I made a 270-degree turn to the left. In so doing, however, they got too far ahead of me and I was unable to catch them.

During the pursuit, however, about fifteen FW 190s became visible climbing toward the bombers from the rear. They were directly in front and about 3,000 feet below me. I picked out the one that appeared to be the highest and made a gentle diving attack on him. When I was about 400 yards astern of him, he dropped his left wing sharply as if he were going to break left. However, by the time I had closed to 200 yards, he leveled off again and was directly in my sights. I closed quickly to about 100 yards and opened fire. I held the burst until I had to break sharply up and to the left to avoid collision. As I broke away, I pulled up sharply to observe the effect of my fire. The FW 190 was streaming flame and smoke from his right wing root and appeared to be in a flat spin around his right landing gear, which had been shot down.

Being all alone and convinced of the Hun's destruction, I proceeded in a direction for home with all possible haste. About one third of the way across the North Sea, I was joined by Lt. Robert S. Johnson of the 61st Fighter Squadron, and we proceeded to the base with no further incident.

Egan had used 444 rounds of .50-caliber ammunition to destroy this FW 190 for his first victory. Egan was able to achieve five victories before his death in combat on July 19, 1944, then commanding the 63rd Fighter Squadron. He is buried in the American Military Cemetery in St Avold/Lorraine, France.

Captain Walker M. Mahurin was leading Postgate Yellow Flight in his P-47C 41-6268. He submitted the following report:

The pilots of the 56th Fighter Group, 63rd Fighter Squadron, posing on
Halesworth. Many of them would fly on August 19 and escort the B-17s on their way
to Gilze-Rijen. Back row, left to right: John D. Wilson, William H. Janson, Frank H.
Peppers, Walter T. Hannigan, Vance P. Ludwig, John H. Truluck, Jack D. Brown,
Raymond D. Petty, and Charles C. Clamp. Middle row, left to right: Wilfred A.
VanAble, Harry P. Dugas, Edgar D. Whitley, Glenn L. Hodges, Gordon E. Batdorf,
Harold E. Comstock, Joseph L. Egan, Pat M. Williams, George A. Compton, and
George F. Hall. Front row, left to right: Lucien A. Dade, John W. Vogt, Wayne J.
O'Connor, Lyle A. Adrianse, Sylvester V. Burke, Philip E. Tukey, Roger B. Dyar,
Walker M. Mahurin, Arthur Sugas, Don M. Goodfleisch, and Glen D. Schlitz.
JOHN H. TRULUCK JR.

Our flight (Captain Mahurin, Lieutenant Ludwig, Lieutenant Vogt,
and Lieutenant Whitley) reached the bombers just east of Woensdrecht at about 1757 hours. We were with them for about five minutes, flying at about 25,000 feet, when we sighted a FW 190 south of
the bombers and 8,000 feet below. I made a long pass, but my speed
was excessive and as a result I was unable to close. I took a snap shot
and pulled back up to the bombers.

We covered the bombers effectively until the group leader
announced we should go home.

We started out heading 320 degrees. As we reached the coast near Walcheren Island, I sighted three Me 109s coming from our left, 1,000 feet below. We made a left turn which brought us behind the 109s and as I got set to shoot them, turned right. I took deflection on the middle Me 109 at about 300 yards and fired a short burst. I was unable to turn with him because of my high speed, so I broke upward and to the left.

Lieutenant Vogt, my second element leader, immediately picked up the lead Me 109 and attacked, shooting it down in flames. Lieutenant Whitley took the third Me 109 and shot it down in flames. I covered them both and then came home with Lieutenant Vogt, while Lieutenant Ludwig brought Lieutenant Whitley back.

First Lieutenant John W. Vogt Jr., flying in P-47C 41-6325, reported on this same fight:

While flying Postgate Yellow 3 position on a B-17 escort mission, our flight encountered three Me 109s preparing to make a head-on attack on the bombers. At that time, the bombers were approximately ten miles from the coast on a course out, while the 109s were just on the coast line, near Walcheren Island, preparing to go in at them. At about 1825 hours, we bounced the enemy from about 21,000 feet and from above, up the sun, so it is doubtful if they saw us before it was too late. I pressed home my attack on one ship, which attempted to evade by breaking left. I fired a short burst in front of him, whereupon he attempted to reverse his turn. This put me right behind him at about 100 yards where a four second burst caused him to explode in a sheet of flame.

In the meantime my wing man, Lieutenant Whitley had singled out another ship and successfully destroyed it. Yellow 1 and 2, Captain Mahurin and Lieutenant Ludwig, who had found it too difficult to turn into the attack at first, due to a high diving speed, effectively covered us during the entire attack and witnessed the whole show.

In all, Vogt had used 673 rounds of .50-caliber ammunition to destroy this Me 109. His wingman, Lt. Edgar D. Whitley, in P-47D 42-7885, reported:

At about 1825 hours, I was flying Postgate Yellow 4, line abreast, at 20,000 feet. We were ten miles ahead of the forts and had just crossed the Dutch coast when Capt. Mahurin sighted three bogeys flying north along the coast. We broke in behind them in a string, then they broke east toward the bombers. As we had come out of the sun it is doubtful that they saw us and broke to make an attack head-on on the bombers. Yellow 3, Lieutenant Vogt, attacked the rear Me 109 on the right and I saw it explode after his first burst.

In the meantime, the northernmost Me 109 was in a position to slide in behind Yellow 3, so I immediately attacked him. I opened fire at 300 yards, thirty-degree deflection, and fired to 50 yards, no deflection. I saw bursts hitting all over the Hun. He took no evasive action other than to climb straight ahead. My tracers hit him from underneath right in the belly. Pieces and smoke flew past me and my canopy was covered with oil as I broke off and returned home.

Whitley had used at least 1,450 rounds from his .50 caliber for the destruction of the second Me 109.

Both Vogt and Whitley had their claims for the destruction of the German fighters confirmed. For Whitley, it was his second and last confirmed air victory. The Me 109 was Vogt's very first victory in air combat. He would continue his markmanship and ended with eight confirmed enemy aircraft destroyed. He obtained his last two victories almost a year later, on August 4,

P-47C 41-6211, in which Capt. Robert A. Lamb claimed to have shot down an Me 109 in the Breda/Moerdijk area around 1825 hours. This P-47 was lost on December 1, 1943. USAAF

1944, then having the rank of major and serving in the 356th Fighter Group. Although their flight leader, Walker M. Mahurin, did not succeed in downing a German fighter this day, he did so on many other occasions. He ended his fighting days against the *Luftwaffe* on March 27, 1944 when he was shot down by the rear gunner of a Dornier 217, with twenty-one confirmed air victories to his credit. (Mahurin then evaded capture, returned to England in May 1944, was repatriated to the United States, and then entered combat in the Southwest Pacific theater of operations, where he added a Japanese bomber to his score.)

The last German fighter that was claimed shot down by the 56th Fighter Group was a victim of Capt. Robert A. Lamb of the 61st Fighter Squadron. He was leading Keyworth Yellow Flight in his P-47C 41-6211. He reported:

> We were at 25,000 feet and inland about 5 miles and still climbing. Four Me 109s came on the left side of our group formation heading in the opposite direction. They then swung around and came up behind my flight. I could not see them, so Blue Flight broke to the left and went down on them at 1805 hours. I saw Capt. Gerald W. Johnson hit one Me 109 which flipped on its back and went straight down trailing some smoke. We circled above the attack. I then heard Blue Leader say to join up above the bombers, which were in their first turn over Gilze-Rijen.
>
> I flew straight to the bombers. My flight was a little strung out and my two and three men got separated from me, due to the attacks by FW 190s. Lieutenant Mudge and I circled above the bombers through their orbit and then followed the box going back over Gilze-Rijen when they separated. We were about 2,000 feet above the bombers, at 22,000 feet. I saw four FW 190s make a raking attack on the bombers left side while going in the opposite direction. They then swung around to come in on the stern of the bombers at the same level. This was about 1820 hours. Lieutenant Mudge followed me down on their tail going inland slightly. Two of the FW 190s broke off to the right and I followed the two going to the left. Lieutenant Mudge about then lost me in the haze. I fired at the second FW 190 at about 300 yards and he rolled over and went down. I then pulled around to the first one and fired at about the same range at him. I saw a small amount of smoke from him. Both were about twenty-degree deflection.
>
> The FW 190 that broke down came back up above me turning to the left. This all was at about 15,000 feet. I zoomed above him back up to about 18,000 feet and got on his tail. I opened fire on him at

about 200 yards and closed to within 50 yards still in a turn to the left. Four more FW 190s came in on me from behind, so I rolled over to the right and started for the deck. As I started to roll over, I looked at the FW 190 which I had been shooting at and he was starting straight down on his back and from the cockpit to the back of the ship was hidden in flame, above which heavy smoke poured.

I then hit the deck with two FW 190s after me near Moerdijk and soon saw Lieutenant Mudge about one half mile to my left also on the deck. We joined up and went out together. About halfway out of the estuary, I saw two gun boats in the water, which were firing at me. I saw his tracers going past my canopy. At the same time I could see cannon strikes in the water in front of me from the FW 190s behind me. I could not get my nose down to fire back at the boats for fear of going into the water. I passed directly above each boat and as close to them as possible. My aircraft suffered no damage. The FW 190s split up and one followed Lieutenant Mudge and one followed me. They were at about 1,000 yards behind us and did not gain or lose. They followed us about ten miles out to sea and then gave up the chase. We came home together on a course of 290 degrees, landing at 1910 hours.

Robert Lamb had used 912 .50-caliber rounds.

Thus, the combat for the 56th Fighter Group ended in a nine-to-one score. The group had shot down nine German fighters and had lost Glenn Hodges, who ditched his Thunderbolt and was captured. However, the loss of the group could easily have been greater. The commanding officer, Col. Hubert Zemke, had nearly been lost to "friendly fire." Zemke, in P-47C 41-6330, was following an FW 190 when an object hit his windshield. He broke off his chase, thinking that pieces were starting to fall from his victim. After his safe return on Halesworth, a .50-caliber bullet was found in his cockpit. Apparently, gunners aboard B-17s had been firing on the FW 190 as well, and did not notice that the plane trailing it was a P-47, instead of another FW 190. It is also possible that Zemke was fired upon by a member of his own group. The FW 190 and the P-47 did much look alike, especially from the front and in combat when split-second decisions had to be made. Zemke, who had replaced a sheet of armoured glass in order to save weight and improve performance of his Thunderbolt, had this quickly replaced after the incident and went on for an impressive career.

The incident also clearly illustrates the dilemma for both the bomber crews and the fighter pilots. In their debriefing reports, almost all bomber crews requested closer escort by fighters. On the other hand, especially the

The damage to the windshield of Zemke's P-47C 41-6330. USAAF

similarity between the FW 190 and the P-47 made them cautious of incoming fighters and sometimes the course of action was "shoot first, ask questions later." This then made the P-47 pilots very wary and they usually preferred staying out of range of the hundreds of .50-caliber machine guns and eager gunners in a B-17 formation. Word spread quickly between the fighter pilots after incidents like that happened to Zemke.

The summary of the successful pilots of the 56th Fighter Group and their claims is as follows:

Johnson, Gerald W.	Capt	Me 109 at 1802 near Gilze-Rijen
Johnson, Robert S.	1st Lt	Me 109 at 1802 north-east of Woensdrecht
McCauley, Frank E.	1st Lt	Me 109 at 1805 near Oosterhout
McCauley, Frank E.	1st Lt	Me 109 at 1810 near Schoonhoven
Quirk, Michael J.	1st Lt	FW 190 at 1810 near Gilze-Rijen
Egan Jr, Joseph L.	1st Lt	FW 190 at 1820 over Tholen
Vogt Jr, John W.	1st Lt	Me 109 at 1825 near Walcheren
Whitley, Edgar D.	1st Lt	Me 109 at 1826 off Walcheren
Lamb, Robert A.	Capt	FW 190 at 1825 north of Breda

Who were the German pilots that suffered from the guns of the 56th Fighter Group? The main problem in identifying the casualties is the absence of a complete German loss list. Not all lost or damaged aircraft were listed in the official records. Very often, pilots bailed out or belly-landed to fight another day and the Germans just didn't bother to list all wrecked or destroyed aircraft. Since the combats on August 19 took place over only a limited area, it has been possible to identify several German crashes by studying records in various Dutch city archives. The data from these Dutch archives, together with those of the official German loss lists, give the best possible loss list (as listed in Appendix A).

The first German fighter to fall was Me 109 *Gelbe 8* of 8./JG 3, based out of Mönchengladbach. It was shot down at 1803 hours and was totally destroyed in the crash near Loon op Zand. The pilot, whose name is not listed in the archives, bailed out unscathed.

Around the same time, *Unteroffizier* Jan Schild of 2./JG 26 belly-landed his FW 190 *Schwarze 7* near Vinkenberg, west of Roosendaal. The plane was 50 percent damaged, but Schild got out safely.

Not so *Leutnant* Leberecht Altmann of 1./JG 26. He crashed with his FW 190 A-5 51091 *Weisse 4* near Eethen. The extent of his injuries is not known, but they were not severe, and he soon returned to duty with his Staffel.

Another unknown German pilot, this time of 7./JG 26 survived the crash of his Me 109 14996 near Brecht, just over the Dutch-Belgian border. The cause of the crash was not listed.

Finally, *Leutnant* Werner Grupe of 12./JG 26 was wounded in the vicinity of Breda in his Me 109 19373 *Schwarze 3*. After recovering from his wounds, he also returned to duty.

Two more German fighters crashed in the general area of Gilze-Rijen, but these two must be attributed to gunners aboard B-17s and will be covered in more detail later. In all, five German losses against nine claims. It is possible that one or more German aircraft crashed off the Dutch coast or in the large estuaries between the Dutch islands and were not listed, but this cannot be ascertained.

So far, we've seen the exploits of the 56th Fighter Group, but what about their brothers-in-arms of the 353rd Fighter Group, who were also scheduled to provide escort for the Gilze-Rijen force. They were less successful. As told before, the unit was only on its fifth escort mission. Up to this day, only one enemy fighter had been destroyed by one of its pilots—and then only by its newly appointed commanding officer, experienced Lt. Col. Loren G. McCollum, on August 17. The pilots of the group were still lacking operational experience and most probably did not have the tactical insight the pilots of the 56th Fighter Group already had gained in the months of combat before.

The 353rd Fighter Group may also have been positioned less favorably in respect to the bombers and the incoming German fighters than the 56th Fighter Group. Its pilots did not succeed in downing a German fighter. Instead, some of them came close to being shot down themselves.

Second Lieutenant Victor L. Vogel of the 352nd Fighter Squadron reported:

> I was flying Wakeford White 4, making a turn to port above Gilze-Rijen airdrome when I heard over the radio, "Wakeford White, break right." I immediately turned right and noticed an unidentified aircraft on my tail closing in on me. I half-rolled and headed for home on the deck. Going out near the bay, I noticed three small boats and opened fire, but could not observe results. A little further on, I met a flak boat that fired on me. I came home on the deck.

Some of the 353rd Fighter Group pilots became involved in dog fights with the German fighter pilots. Capt. Walter C. Beckham of the 351st Fighter Squadron reported:

> After bombers had made their turn toward home, I observed five or six enemy aircraft attacking the second box that we were escorting from head-on. My flight went down after the last two of these. We were observed by the two Me 109s, who made a sharp turn to the left and then started going straight down doing rolls to the left. I came into very good range at first, but was not able to turn enough to get sufficient lead, so did not fire. I did fire a couple of short bursts (twenty-one rounds out of each gun) as we were going straight down, but doubt them having had any accuracy, due to the violent maneuvers the enemy aircraft were making. Pulling out with the Me 109 that I was chasing, turning still slightly inside of me, and pulling out at the same time. He could have gotten a shot at me, as I overshot on the pull out, but apparently did not see me for he made no effort to make the right turn that might have placed him on my tail. I pulled out at about 10,000 feet and climbed back up slowly to 20,000 feet on my way out. My wingman, Lieutenant Morris, followed us down also and stated that he fired a burst at extreme range. He went down to the deck after the engagement and went home at minimum altitude. I joined other P-47s at the coast and came back with them.

His wingman, 2nd Lt. Harold J. Morris, described this fight:

We sighted several enemy aircraft attacking bombers and went
down after last two of these. I was on the left and turning left, trying
to get in position to fire on the Me 109. I first, at about 1,200 yards,
fired a short burst. I closed in and fired another burst at about 100
yards and forty-five-degree deflection, just as the enemy aircraft was
rolling over on his back. The Me 109 continued over on his back
and headed straight down. Since I was at 9,000 feet, I hit the deck
and came home. On the way out, I fired at what appeared to be a
factory and also at some tanks.

Although no hits were visible in his exposed gun-camera film, he was
awarded the Me 109 as "damaged," probably on account of his combat
report.

Despite that, he was not so lucky on this day, Beckham would soon do
better. When he was shot down by light flak on February 22, 1944, he had
achieved a total of eighteen enemy aircraft destroyed in aerial combat and
was, at that time, the leading ace of the Eighth Air Force. Neither Vogel nor
Morris was able to shoot down German fighters during their remaining
combat missions.

The 56th Fighter Group had given especially good account of itself and
had spoiled many attacks by German fighters on the B-17 formations. The

On the left is Maj. John C. Bishop, who led the 103rd Composite Combat Wing to
Gilze-Rijen. GEORGE P. BIRDSONG

flights of the group had become dispersed and the fighters were low on fuel, so they had to return to Halesworth. In the after-action report of the 56th Fighter Group, the following recommendation was made: "It cannot be expected that fighters can stay with the bombers when they change their plans and orbit to find other targets. This point must be impressed on them."

It is now time to look at the exploits of these bomber crews again and see why this remark found its place in the report.

We have left the bombers over the North Sea, approaching the Dutch coast. Major John C. Bishop and Capt. Harry T. Lay, leading not only the planes of their 91st Bomb Group, but those of the entire combat wing in *Oklahoma Okie*, reported on the next episode:

> We picked up P-47 escort at approximately the initial point. This I.P. was covered with a layer of stratus at about 10,000 feet and target was not picked up until about forty seconds before time of release. The bombardier's gyroscope was upset and a second run was necessary. Fighters were encountered after turning off the target and P-47s were observed attacking them although the formation did receive intermittent attacks. We made a large circle to the left and came back on target with only about a ten second bomb run. Turned off the target the second time and left coast as briefed, thirteen minutes behind flight plan.

The decision not to bomb on the first run over the target became the subject of many profanities aboard the other ships in the formation. The bomber crews knew that their fighter escort now could not stay with them for the entire time over enemy territory as planned. The return trip for the bombers was now to be unescorted and just two days earlier they had paid a high price for that. In view of this recent experience, especially for the 91st and 381st Bomb Groups, the 360-degree turn demonstrates a true devotion to duty of the group leaders. Nothing would have been easier for Bishop and Lay than to drop their bombs on the first run, regardless of the problems that the bombardier was having, and head home. It must have been a very tempting thing to do, but instead, they chose to make another bomb run and to do the utmost to get their bombs on the target, in spite of the increased risks to themselves and their command.

It is unfortunate that because of the chaotic assembly and the odd four-squadron formation of the group no proper radio contact between the squadron leaders was ever established. Bishop was now unable to communicate that a second run would be made. The only clue for the other squadrons that there was to be such a second run was that no bombs tumbled out of the opened bomb bays of the 91st Bomb Group's ships.

Flying as lead navigator for the low squadron, furnished by the 381st Bomb Group, was 1st Lt. Leonard L. Spivey. He recalls this episode:

On the approach to the target, ground characteristics could be distinguished with reasonable certainty. There were some haze and smoke screens visible, but the I.P. and the target were clearly identifiable. I pointed out the I.P. to 2nd Lt. Edward T. O'Loughlin, our bombardier, and confirmed that he spotted the target. There was a rule in Bomber Command that when bombing in occupied countries, the specific target must be visible and identifiable—otherwise, you did not drop your bombs. In other words, there was to be no guess work that might unduly risk civilians. While there was no real problem with visibility in this case, surprisingly, the wing leader, for some unfathomable reason, either aborted the bomb run or simply did not drop, and then proceeded in a left turn, which ended up as a 360-degree. Our composite group, as per procedure, maintained position in formation and followed second timer around. There was gab on the intercom: "Now we're sitting ducks!"

Upon return to Ridgewell later that evening, there also was much criticism among the crews for not bombing on the first run, as most bombardiers said they had clearly identified the target then. However, O'Loughlin, had correctly followed the standard operational procedure and had waited for the group lead bombardier on *Oklahoma Okie* to bomb.

However, despite this procedure, which was also already mentioned by Spivey above, the other two squadrons in the lead group had dropped their bombs on the first run over the target anyhow. One was the high squadron furnished by the 351st Bomb Group. Captain Robert H. Johnson, leading this squadron, reported rather dryly: "An uneventful trip to the target was made and as my bombardier was sighting for range and the group leader was to take care of course, we dropped our bombs on the first run. We made another run over the target and the rest of the group (lead and low squadrons) then dropped their bombs."

Dropping at the same time as this high squadron was the stray squadron of the 379th Bomb Group, which had squeezed itself into the wing formation. In some of the strike pictures taken by a bomb-bay camera of one of the planes of the 351st Bomb Group, even a plane of the 379th Bomb Group can be seen. Second Lieutenant Kenneth L. Johnson, the lead bombardier of this squadron, put down his experiences, too:

I pinpointed all the way in to the target. We were briefed for an indicated altitude of 20,000 feet, but the group we joined went to an indicated altitude of 21,500 feet. The data we had could not be changed in the air and I wasn't sure of the group we had joined as to the kind of bombs they had, so I figured if I aimed 500 yards short and used the data we had been briefed on, we would hit the target. I did not observe the results of the bombing due to the fact that I had some hung bombs and I had to salvo. After the turn, I went back to the bomb bay and threw out loose bombs in the bomb bay. In the meantime, the group had gone over the target again. We encountered flak on the second run of the target. I sighted for range only.

When we look at the results of the bombs of these two squadrons, it seems to have been a very wise decision for Edward O'Loughlin not to drop on the first run as well. In his report, 1st Lt. Stanley Taylor, the lead bombardier of the 351st Bomb Group's squadron, blamed the lead squadron with setting up an improper course, forcing him to the right and thus dropping to the right of the aiming point.

The result of this first run was that the bombs of both squadrons had overshot the target a little to the right and had hit several farms in Hulten, northeast of the airfield, and the rural area around it. Furthermore, bombs exploded across the railroad running from Breda to Tilburg. Results of the 168 100-pound general-purpose bombs dropped by the planes of the 351st Bomb Group and the 1,138 lethal twenty-pound fragmentation bombs by those of the 379th Bomb Group were disastrous for the Dutch civilian population. Twenty-three civilians, first anxiously watching the American formations overhead, were killed. Many others were injured in and near Hulten. The experience of the civil population is recorded in the next chapter.

Now the entire group made the large left turn that was initiated aboard *Oklahoma Okie* and headed for the airfield again. This turn took them over Oosterhout, Zevenbergen, and Roosendaal and then over the original initial point to the target again. This turn took the formation about ten minutes. One can only imagine how the wounded and badly shaken population of Hulten must have felt by seeing a formation of bombers approaching them again. This time the squadrons of the 91st and 381st Bomb Group in the lead group dropped their bombs. These hit the airfield in the northeastern corner, hitting at least one hangar with an Me 110 night-fighter of I./NJG 1 in or near it. Both the hangar and the fighter caught fire and were totally destroyed. Probably some of these bombs overshot into the already hit area

The bomb-bay camera of B-17F 42-29749 *Belle of the Bayous* of the 351st Bomb Group captured the unfolding tragedy in Hulten. Here the bombs have been released over the village of Gilze. In the top righthand corner is Gilze-Rijen airfield. USAAF

in Hulten, although this cannot be ascertained on the strike pictures that were taken. In all, the 91st Bomb Group had dropped 1,110 twenty-pound fragmentation bombs and the 381st Bomb Group 111 100-pound general-purpose bombs.

Half the load on B-17F 42-5178 *The Old Stand By* of the 91st Bomb Group hung up over the target. These twelve cluster bombs, containing

In the next picture (the right of the first picture shows the same terrain as the left of the second), the bombs have overshot the airfield to the right and start exploding in and around Hulten, between the main Breda-Tilburg road and the railway line. USAAF

seventy-two of the smaller fragmentation bombs, were later salvoed. Two crews of the 381st Bomb Group also experienced problems during the final bomb run. On B-17F 42-29888 *The Joker*, mechanical difficulties prevented the release of all its twenty-four bombs; they stayed in the bomb bay for the return trip. On B-17F 42-29988 *Lucifer Jr*, nine bombs hung up in the racks and were also taken back toward Ridgewell.

The third picture shows the numerous bursts caused by the smaller fragmenta-
tion bombs, even across the railway line. Note a B-17 of the 379th Bomb
Group, which had also bombed on this run, slowly drifting toward the 351st
Bomb Group formation. USAAF

Now the formation took up course for England again. The four
squadrons almost had escaped all attention by the *Luftwaffe*. However, a little south of Rotterdam, several German fighters appeared, which made
brief attacks on the formation. Only one aircraft in the lead squadron sustained damage by this attack, B-17F 42-5763 *Bomb-Boogie* of the 91st Bomb
Group was hit in the vertical fin by a 20mm cannon shell. Two German

In the final picture, this plane is in full view. On the far left are more exploding bombs. Running through the middle of the picture is the Wilhelmina canal.
USAAF

fighters, an Me 109 and FW 190, were claimed destroyed by the group's gunners. The first was claimed by Sgt. James H. Witter, the right waist gunner of B-17F 42-5178 *The Old Stand By*: "At 1824 hours, two enemy aircraft were coming in at the squadron below at four o'clock and about 500 feet below this aircraft. I began firing when the enemy aircraft were about 500 yards off and fired about sixty rounds at the leader. One of the enemy aircraft began to burn violently and went into an uncontrolled dive and crashed on to the ground below."

The FW 190 was claimed by Sgt. Edward Kistojewski, the right waist gunner of B-17F 42-3079: "At 1826 hours, two FWs came in at two o'clock a little below. I opened fire at 400 yards and held on him as he came in and turned away toward four o'clock and at 450 yards he exploded like a sky rocket and there was just little pieces of flaming parts. Both tail gunner and ball turret gunner saw the plane explode."

From the right waist gun position of the 91st Bomb Group's *Oklahoma Okie*, observer Maj. William M. Jackson took this picture (and the two that follow) of B-17F 42-5763 *Bomb-Boogie* dropping its bombs over Gilze-Rijen. In the first picture are flak bursts close to the nose. CHAUNCEY H. HICKS

In the second picture, the bomb-bay doors are opened. In the background, two B-17s can be seen. CHAUNCEY H. HICKS

In the third picture, the bombs are dropped, and the ball turret gunner has turned his turret forward to observe the drop and check that all bombs properly leave the ship. The first clusters of fragmentation bombs can already be seen breaking up in the air. *Bomb-Boogie* was lost on the mission to Stuttgart on September 6, 1943.
CHAUNCEY H. HICKS

Both were confirmed as destroyed by 1st Bomb Wing Headquarters. Although no planes in the squadrons of the 351st and 379th Bomb Groups, sustained battle damage by these attacks, 351st Bomb Group's gunners claimed no less than five German fighters destroyed. Three German fighters are known to have crashed or belly-landed along the route taken by the Americans after the target. More about this later in this chapter.

The low squadron received most attention from the enemy fighters. These seven ships of the 381st Bomb Group were led by 1st Lt. Orlando H. Koenig and 2nd Lt. Joseph L. Mangarpan in B-17F 42-3101. The bomber belonged to the 535rd Bomb Squadron and its fuselage code was MS-T. The crew was not a regular combat crew, but was a composite crew from two different squadrons, the 533rd and 535th—no doubt caused by the grievous losses the 381st Bomb Group suffered two days earlier over Schweinfurt.

Second Lieutenant William F. Cormany, Jr., was piloting B-17F 42-29988 *Lucifer Jr* and reported after landing on Ridgewell:

> We had made the second run on the target, dropped our bombs and turned on course to return to England. My position in the formation was number three in the second element of the low

squadron, low group. The formation met attacks by enemy aircraft and during an attack from nine o'clock level, Lieutenant Koenig's aircraft was hit, evidently by 20mm cannon fire. I saw the number three gas tank and, soon, the entire inboard sector of the right wing burning furiously. The aircraft was definitely still under the control of the pilot or co-pilot as it left the formation in an easy, slightly diving turn to the right, turning back into enemy-occupied territory. The tail gunner of my aircraft, Staff Sgt. Frank C. Rumberger, reported seeing himself six parachutes from Lieutenant Koenig's aircraft. Because it was so well under control, it is my opinion that all uninjured personnel on board should have parachuted safely.

The pilot of B-17F 42-30034 *Nobody's Baby* was 1st Lt. Dexter Lishon:

Aircraft 42-3101 piloted by Lieutenant Koenig was last seen leaving the formation under control in a gliding turn to the right. His number three engine was on fire and six parachutes were seen before the plane went out of sight of our formation. He was headed back into Holland.

The cause of this plane's destruction was enemy aircraft. Three FW 190s with checker board noses came in from eleven o'clock from the sun. It did not appear as if any other ship in the formation was firing on them, except mine [number two, second element], because of the glare from the sun. The enemy aircraft shot over the cockpit and got the number three engine. One seemed to get him from above while another was a little bit lower and got him from below. [Cormany and Lishon and their crews were among the seven crews the 381st Bomb Group lost during the mission to Bremen on October 8, 1943.]

The German fighters that brought about the destruction belonged to the First Gruppe of Jagdgeschwader 1, based on Deelen airfield. It was *Leutnant* Georg Schott of 1./JG 1, who was credited with shooting down the B-17. Its navigator was 1st Lt. Leonard L. Spivey, who recalls:

Our aircraft had already taken flak hits in the right wing, at or near numbers three and four engines, while we were over the target area. Fuel was seen streaming out of large holes in the wing. Then shortly after turning away from the target and heading northwest, we spotted three or four fighters flying abreast at nine o'clock. They were out of range, and anyway at that distance we were not sure whether

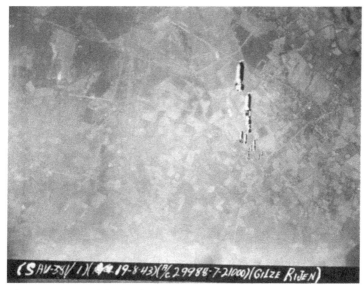

The second run of the lead group, as captured by the camera aboard B-17F 42-29988 *Lucifer Jr* of the 381st Bomb Group, flown by 2nd Lt. William F. Cormany Jr. In this picture, the bombs are released over the village of Gilze. The target is visible at the top of the picture. USAAF

The next photo shows the cloud of smoke and dust caused by the bombs that have been dropped on the first run by the ships of the 351st and 379th Bomb Groups. USAAF

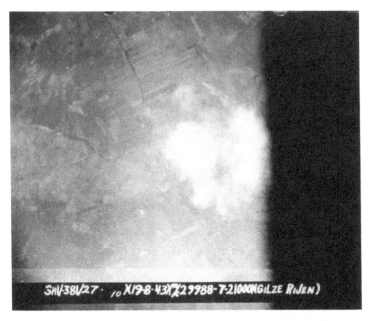

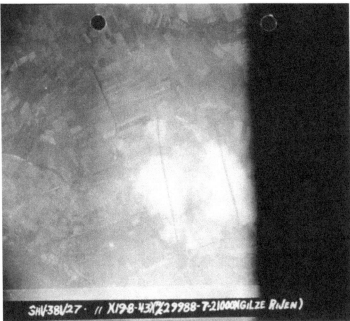

The third and fourth frames show the area where the bombs of the 91st and 381st Bomb Group hit, as indicated with pencil marks by an intelligence officer on Ridgewell. Note some plainly visible burning farms and hay stacks in Hulten. USAAF

they were friend or foe. They skirted ahead, and as anticipated they suddenly turned toward the formation from a slightly higher level and more or less head on. They were FW 190s!! Two of them coming from eleven o'clock were heading directly for our aircraft. Their wings were flashing with 20mm cannon fire. As happens with a head-on attack, the closure was so fast we were only able to get off a few short bursts before they zoomed under us, rolled and dove away.

We were hit! Immediately there was a dense smoke filling the nose compartment and an acrid smell was coming through my oxygen mask. I reported the situation to Koenig, the pilot. His instant response was "Bail out!"

"Did you say bail out?"

"Yes, bail out! Bail out!"

I motioned to the bombardier and saw that he understood the order. The right wing was on fire at numbers three and four engines. I pulled off my intercom wires and oxygen mask and proceeded to the bottom hatch door, aft of my compartment. The bombardier had left the nose and was behind me. I was squatting in

Four men of this replacement crew for the 533rd Bomb Squadron of the 381st Bomb Group were aboard B-17F 42-3101 when it was shot down south of Rotterdam on August 19. Standing second from left is 2nd Lt. Edward T. O'Loughlin (bombardier, POW), and second from right is 2nd Lt. Joseph L. Mangarpan Jr. (copilot, POW). Kneeling, first and second from right, respectively, are Staff Sgt. Eugene A. Sabourin (tail gunner, KIA) and Tech Sgt. Russell G. Chester (radio operator, POW). JOSEPH L. MANGARPAN

front of the hatch ready to pull the red emergency release on the hinge side of the door, when Koenig appeared in the hatchway from the pilot's compartment. I nodded; he nodded. I quickly pulled the release and gave the door a solid kick in the middle. It fell away easily, and I watched it tumble down and aft seemingly fast. The bombardier was close behind me by then. I folded my arms firmly in front of my chest pack and from the squatting position dove or rolled head-first out the small opening, less than two feet square, I believe. The next thing I was aware of was hanging in the harness with a painful tight pressure in the pelvis area, caused by the pull of the leg straps.

Many Dutch civilians were eyewitness to the events in the air. One of them was sixteen-year-old Arie de Jong, who lived in Vlaardingen. He kept a wartime diary and recorded the events.

1930 hours (German time, one hour ahead of British Summer Time). Another formation passes overhead, now about thirty planes, all B-17s. At the same time the air raid sirens are sounded and concentrated flak is fired. Some German fighters try to close in on the bombers. One fighter is shot down, the others flee.

Suddenly, a flash, followed by black smoke, comes from one of the Flying Fortresses. Apparently the flak has struck, the plane leaves the formation in a southerly direction. A wing breaks off between the engines, but the main spar of the wing prevents the part from falling off. At about 2,500 meters the plane enters a spin. Until about 1,000 meters, the wing remains attached to the plane, but then breaks off. The plane somersaults, enters a spin again, and falls to the ground. At the time when the plane entered its first spin, white dots are visible in the air. At first, we think they are explosions, then balloons. As they descend, we can see that they are six parachutes. It takes them about fifteen minutes to reach the ground. All this takes to about 1950 hours.

Second Lieutenant Joseph L. Mangarpan, the copilot, remembers this episode:

Koenig gave the order to bail out. By the time I got to the hatch beneath the pilots compartment, both Spivey and O'Loughlin had gone. The hatch was open, I snapped on my chest pack chute and tumbled out. I don't remember pulling the rip cord; the next thing

Deelen airfield, June 1943. *Leutnant* Georg Schott and *Leutnant* Rudolf Engleder of 1./JG 1 in full flying gear. Both claimed a B-17 destroyed, at 1921 and 1922 hours, respectively, in the vicinity of Rozenburg and Moerdijk. This was B-17F 42-3101 of the 381st Bomb Group. ROB W. DE VISSER

I remember was floating down and the eerie quietness, not a sound to be heard other than the rustle of the canopy of the chute. Evidently, when I jumped, my harness was loose and my testicles were jammed between my legs; it hurt a great deal and I remember trying to climb up shroud lines to release the pressure, but no luck. At one point, I saw a German fighter heading for me. All I could think about was getting shot, we had heard stories of that happening, but all the pilot of the fighter did was pass close to me. I could see him in his cockpit and he threw me a salute, which was a great relief at that point. After floating for what seemed like hours due to the pressure on my groin, I saw the ground approaching rather fast. I hit hard on my right foot in a ploughed field. I lay a few minutes in great pain in my right foot, but the pressure on my groin was gone at that moment. Then I saw a person dressed in a black suit coming to my aid. When he arrived, he was pleasant and tried to help me to my feet. With much effort, I finally was able to stand and hobble on my left leg along with him, heading for a barn or house. He made a gesture of friendship and said, "You are safe now." I'll never forget the great feeling of relief. We hobbled to the building and I sat down. There was a woman there and she said, "Milk, milk," and I said, "Yes." She brought a large pitcher of cold milk and I proceeded to drink it with great relish. After a few minutes, we heard the sound of a motor and "Achtung Achtung." At that moment, I knew it was over; a German officer came into the room and wanted to know who I was and questioned me about a pistol, which I didn't carry. He was satisfied at this point and ordered a private to pick me up and place me in a staff car, as I indicated my right leg was hurt. From here, we went on to Rotterdam.

Navigator Leonard Spivey, floating down with a painful pelvis, resumes his account:

After bailing out, I was never able to spot my aircraft or, for that matter, the formation itself. The large sheepskin collar of the B-3 flight jacket had been pushed up around the back of my head and ears by the riser straps as the chute opened, and they more of less secured the collar in that position during the entire descent. Vision was consequently limited to about 180 degrees forward unless I twisted rather awkwardly in the harness. I was facing northerly, the same direction as my drift. Swinging back and forth, north to south, at about a 40-degree arc, I seemed to feel a sudden drop on the back swing and hear a "whoosh" and a flap of the fabric. There was a momentary concern about the chute folding at the top of the swing. Right at first, I had been aware of the bomber formation by the sound of the fading drone of its engines, and the distant explosions of anti-aircraft shells. Far below, through the ground haze and streams of smoke, I saw muzzle flashes of the flak guns and heard the shells as they tunneled through the atmosphere. Then after a while, it was quiet except for the occasional flap of the fabric—almost peaceful.

At about midway in descent, a pair of Me 109s came in sight from the north-east and headed straight for me. The scare stories I had heard in the Nissen huts back at the base instantly came to mind. Afraid of being used for target practice, I was getting ready to try to spill my chute and make a tougher target, but just about then, the fighters veered slightly away to the right and flew by very closely. I could see the pilot's faces looking at me. They wiggled their wings. I returned the salute with considerable relief.

Debriefing on Ridgewell, July or August 1943. On the far left is 1st Lt. Leonard L. Spivey, who was shot down on August 19 and landed in Schiedam. LEONARD L. SPIVEY

Closer to the ground, it was clear that I would be landing in a heavily built up area. Many buildings, tall stacks and railway tracks were visible as well as many canals and larger waterways. At about 2,000 feet I could see a maze of power lines and poles. I thought of the warning to cross the feet in the event of going on to the wires, which it was better to glance off than straddle going some ten to fifteen miles per hour.

I heard many strident voices coming from below. People had seen me. Crowds of faces were looking up. I saw the buildings, lines and poles coming up. I pulled on the risers, I think the swinging stopped then. Everything was rushing up fast now. Facing in the direction of ground travel, with legs slightly flexed, my feet hit and I tumbled forward. Somehow I had missed the obstructions and landed in a grassy area next to a railroad station. Now on my back, I quickly turned the release knob and hit it. The trusty RAF chute harness fell away. A quick glance around: uniformed men were running toward me. In a silly attempt to hide, I rolled into a shallow ditch nearby. This must have looked pretty comical to the German soldiers and sailors, only a few yards away. One of them raised a "potato masher" grenade above his head and yelled, "Hände auf! Hände auf! Haben Sie eine Pistole?" I got up slowly from the ditch with hands raised and told them I had no weapon. The parachute was gathered up by one of the soldiers and he carried the disarrayed bundle in front of his chest and marched along proudly with all the others.

The now pilotless B-17 crashed near Oud-Rozenburg, south of Rotterdam. The main part of the plane came down in a field east of the Langenlaan, two hundred meters south of the farm of Jacob de Jong. The bodies of four crewmembers were found in the wreckage. They were those of ball turret gunner Staff Sgt. Walter J. Buran, waist gunner Staff Sgt. Wilbert G. Jones, tail gunner Staff Sgt. Eugene A. Sabourin, and a fourth who was not identified at that time. What happened in the rear of the aircraft is recalled by Tech Sgt. Russell G. Chester, the radio operator:

Smoke began to enter the radio room through the open gun hatch. There had been almost no conversation on the intercom, but tail gunner Sabourin broke in to ask if the aircraft was on fire. I told him I thought so because of the smoke in the radio room. Things

First Lt. Orlando H. Koenig, pilot of B-17F 42-3101 of the 381st Bomb Group.
KRISTINE KOENIG

began to happen very quickly now, for just as we were being attacked from the rear to seven o'clock high, the order from up front came: "Bail out, bail out." That was all there was ever said so far as I know, for immediately I disconnected my electrical equipment (throat-mike, earphones, etc.) and put on my parachute. I noticed the waist gunners doing the same. The last thing I did was remove my oxygen mask. The waist gunners had not yet opened their escape hatch. Of course, I could not see Sabourin in the tail and the ball turret was stopped in a position where the gunner could neither come up into the plane, or drop out if he was wearing his chute.

Upon removing my oxygen mask, I made my way quickly to the waist gun positions. The escape door was still in place, so I pulled the handle and kicked the door off the fuselage. The waist gunners still wore their oxygen masks and seemed fascinated by the fire coming from number three engine. I pointed to the open exit and waved for them to come on. They nodded their heads in the affirmative. I jumped and I never saw either of them again.

Staff Sgt. Arthur L. Everett, waist gunner of B-17F 42-3101 of the 381st Bomb Group.
LARRY D. HUTCHINGS

Chester was also quickly captured after his landing. After a few days, he was reunited with engineer Tech Sgt. Leo I. Perkins, who told him the fate of his best friend Eugene Sabourin and the other three gunners.

Perkins later wrote:

I was the last to leave the plane, as far as I know. I was captured next morning, near Rotterdam, and I suppose our plane crashed nearby.

That evening the Germans came to the place they were holding me in a pickup and there were four caskets or coffins in the rear. They put me in the back with a guard and we went to Rotterdam to a cemetery that had a large iron gate and high brick or stone wall. We drove near a building in the cemetery and they made me help unload the four coffins. One of the guards that was in front seat of the pickup had a large envelope and when I was taken to a garrison for the night a German officer showed me three dogtags. They were Jones, Buran, and Sabourin's. There was none for Everett, but I believe all were killed in the plane when it crashed and Everett did not have his dogtags.

Indeed, after the war, the fourth body was positively identified as that of Staff Sgt. Arthur L. Everett, the other waist gunner. The cemetery to which Perkins accompanied the four bodies was Crooswyck in Rotterdam. After the war, the four men were reinterred in the American Military Cemetery in Margraten, the Netherlands. Several years later, Eugene Sabourin's remains were brought back to the United States, where they now rest in a cemetery

Staff Sgt. Eugene A. Sabourin, tail gunner of B-17F 423-3101 of the 381st Bomb Group, and his fiancée in the early spring of 1943. RUSSELL G. CHESTER

in his home state of Massachusetts. The other three are still buried in Margraten.

Russell Chester recalls: "Perkins informed me that Sabourin, Buran, Everett, and Jones had not survived. I had been certain the two waist gunners would survive and had hoped that tail gunner and my best friend Eugene Sabourin would have also somehow survived. Even today, I have difficulty accepting the reality of the situation. For me there is no apparent or plausible reason for the waist gunners' failure to jump."

All six survivors of the crew were made prisoners of war and spent the remainder of the war in various camps. Their capture had resulted in an anti-German demonstration by the civilians of Schiedam. In its monthly intelligence report, the German 376th Infantry Division reported: "When in Schiedam a crewmember of an English plane was led away, the civilian population showed a very supportive attitude toward him, despite the still ongoing air-raid alarm. They crowded around the prisoner of war, tried to shake his hands and said words to the effect that he should try to escape or that others might help him with that. Two men and one women were arrested."

That crewmember probably was Leonard Spivey, who recalls this episode:

> I was escorted across the tracks by the station and into the main street. I saw the sign on the station: SCHIEDAM. There were curious crowds all around, mostly civilians who were waved off by my captors. One very old, frail looking grey haired lady, dressed in black, came toward me and said something in Dutch. From the couple of words I did catch, she must have thought I was British. Anyway, she was obviously a friend—not an enemy. One of the guards pushed her out of the way. Determined, she walked toward me again, with arms outstretched. This time she was handled in a rougher manner and knocked to the pavement.
>
> I was marched down the middle of the street surrounded by a dozen or so armed German military, a mix of *Luftwaffe*, army, and navy. Dutch policemen were holding back the crowd lining the sidewalks. Many people were hanging out of the upper storey windows. Women were waving, especially the younger ones. Some intrepid men, in an attempted "cloaked" fashion, gave me a Churchillian "V" for Victory, with signalling fingers held to their sides or simply resting them on their chin. Others nodded or winked to give me a sign of support.

The Germans were strict in their dealing with this obvious pro-American behavior. The city of Schiedam was fined 100,000 Dutch guilders, and the nightcurfew for its inhabitants was put forward to eight o'clock for a three-week period.

The only other bomber in the low squadron that sustained battle damage from the German fighter attack was B-17F 42-30009 *Feather Merchant*. One assailant was claimed shot down by the squadron's gunners.

Since the German fighters had left by now, an uneventful return flight across the North Sea followed. The bombs which had hung up on *Lucifer Jr* and *The Joker* of the 381st Bomb Group were now dumped in the North Sea. After reaching the wing dispersal point over England at 1918 hours, a 360-degree turn to the left was made to get under clouds, and then the four squadrons took up course to their respective home bases, Bassingbourn, Polebrook, Kimbolton, and Ridgewell and landed about thirty minutes later.

Now we go back in time and return to the 303rd Bomb Group, which we left when it was trailing Lay's lead group at the initial point.

Leading the twenty ships of this group were Maj. William R. Calhoun, Jr., and Capt. Glynn F. Shumake in B-17F 41-24635 *The 8 Ball Mk II*. Calhoun, who had come over to England with the 303rd Bomb Group in October 1942, would fly his twenty-fifth and therefore final combat mission he was required to fly. The copilot of his original crew, 1st Lt. James S. Nix, was scheduled to fly his twenty-fourth mission this day. He was flying with the crew of 2nd Lt. Daniel A. Shebeck and leading the group's low squadron. Their ship for the mission was B-17F 42-3192. In this same ship, most of the crew had flown two days earlier together with their commanding officer, Col. Kermit D. Stevens, leading the 303rd Bomb Group on the Schweinfurt mission.

The first part of the story is best described by the report of Calhoun:

We were at 19,000 feet, and the lead group was at 21,000 feet. We crossed the enemy coast on time, but fighter escort did not show up. Only a few P-47s were seen and these were high and left us as such as we approached the target area. We headed for the I.P., the lead group made a left turn a little beyond the I.P., did not open bomb doors, nor fire I.P. flares.

So we continued a little beyond the I.P., shot flares, opened doors and turned back towards the target. Our turn was late and we were headed so that ground haze and sun prevented us from picking out the target and dropping our bombs. So we closed our doors, made a slight right turn, and fell back into wing formation. The

On August 12, William Calhoun and James Nix flew their last combat mission together in B-17F 41-24635 *The 8 Ball Mk II*. Exactly a week later, Calhoun would lead the 303rd Bomb Group again, this time to Gilze-Rijen in this same aircraft and with all of the enlisted men in this picture. James Nix was flying with the crew of Daniel Shebeck that day and was shot down and killed in action. Standing, from left to right: Flight Off. Harold S. Bolsover (not on mission), Staff Sgt Paul C. Lemann (ball turret gunner), 1st Lt. James S. Nix (copilot), Capt. Robert J. Yonkman (not on mission), Tech Sgt. Arnold S. Doran (engineer), and Staff Sgt. Lloyd L. Jordan (waist gunner). Kneeling, from left to right: Staff Sgt. Paul P. McGee (radio operator), Capt. Joseph M. Strickland (navigator, not on mission), Maj. William R. Calhoun (pilot), and Staff Sgt Joseph Kerr (waist gunner). Note the covered Norden bombsight in the plexiglass nose. PAUL C. LEMANN

combat wing made a tight 360-degree turn to the left and we came back, but before we could pick up target we were over the I.P. again, so the 303rd Bomb Group swung out a little to the right, turned left to come back over the target, and this time we were headed almost directly into the sun. While we were turning toward the target, the other groups had headed for home, making no other bomb run. On our bomb run, the bombardier could not find the target because of sun glare and lead ship did not drop bombs. Some ships in our group dropped bombs. By this time, the other groups had gotten about ten to fifteen miles ahead of us, leaving us all alone. About this time, enemy fighters hit us, and we had no fighter support.

Here again there was much criticism aboard the other bombers for making a second run. But again, credit is due to the perseverance of the group leaders, who didn't want to dump their bombs without proper sighting of the target. However, the price the 303rd Bomb Group had to pay for this turn was heavy.

Just returned from the Antwerp mission of April 5, 1943, are Maj. William Calhoun and film star Clark Gable. The latter took part in a number of combat missions for the movie *Combat America*. CHARLES R. TERRY

The turn of the 303rd Bomb Group took them also over Oosterhout, Zevenbergen, and Roosendaal, but where the lead group had turned sharply toward the target at the I.P., the 303rd had executed a somewhat wider turn and now made its final approach toward the target coming from Tilburg. As Calhoun already indicated in his report, this had the unfortunate effect that they were now heading directly into the sun, which was already low in the sky at this time of day, and this increased the problems for the bombardiers. They not only had to cope with the ground haze and the low sun, but also with the smoke of the bombing of the lead group. In all, 240 100-pound general-purpose bombs were dropped by ten out of the twenty ships in the formation. Strike pictures indicated that the point of release was just over the western outskirts of Tilburg. However, all bombs fell short, no hits were registered on the airfield. Again a rural area was hit, this time a little to the east of the airfield. Luckily, this time there were no civilian casualties on the ground.

As we have already seen, while the 103rd Combat Wing was milling around Gilze-Rijen, their American fighter escort had been busily engaging the about 130 German fighters, which had assembled upon command of the Jagdführer Holland-Ruhr.

After it had bombed Gilze-Rijen on its second prolonged run, which took about fourteen minutes' extra flying time, the 303rd Bomb Group turned to follow its original flight plan and were now struck by German fighters, which either had eluded the American fighters or had simply waited for these to withdraw. No more friendly escort was available. The 303rd Bomb Group, which had lost the connection with the lead group in its larger turn toward the target, was now flying on its own, heading north over North-Brabant.

The *Luftwaffe* took this opportunity and struck the formation with all it had left after the dogfights with the Thunderbolts. Furious battles ensued, the gunners aboard the Fortresses firing back with all available machine guns on the attacking German fighters. Thousands of rounds were spent in the defence of the twenty ships of the 303rd Bomb Group, half of which were still loaded with bombs. Some of these rounds struck home. Flying in Me 109 G-6 16394 *Gelbe 12* of 9./JG 26 was *Feldwebel* Werner Möszner. He recalled:

> After our "alarm start" from Schiphol, I flew as wingman to my *Staffelkapitän*, *Oberleutnant* Paul Schauder. At about 6,000 meters altitude, we first sighted the enemy formation. It consisted of B-17s; we did not see any escorting fighters. During our first attack from the stern, and still at a distance of about 1,200 meters (I had not even opened fire yet), my plane was hit in the oil cooler. My cockpit wind

03/162 - 2)(19·AUG·43· 18:17)(l/c 42·5264 - 12°·18,800') GILZE - RIJEU

First Lt. Louis M. Benepe's *Yankee Doodle Dandy* has just salvoed its lethal cargo of twenty-four 100-pound general-purpose bombs over the western edge of Tilburg. Under the bombs, the railway line from Tilburg to Baarle-Nassau, with its branch to Goirle, is clearly visible. USAAF

V-303/162- 9)(19-AUG-43- 18:17)(W 42-52 64- 12"-18,800') GILZE-RIJ

After a short time (the bottom of the second picture shows the same area as the top of the first picture), the bombs burst in the open fields to the east of Gilze-Rijen airfield. Clearly visible on this picture is the haze that prevented proper sighting of the target. The heavy smoke in the top righthand corner of the picture was caused by the burning hangar on Gilze-Rijen airfield and the bombs that had hit Hulten some ten minutes earlier. USAAF

screen was immediately covered with oil. I tried to use the wipers to get some sight, but this was unsuccessful. I then threw off my cockpit roof. With hand gestures, I motioned to Schauder that I was not wounded. The engine quit completely, the propellor stopped. I orientated myself, saw large rivers, didn't really think about bailing out and decided to make a belly landing. My forward view was miserable, and because of the rush of the wind, the side view was hampered as well. That's why I didn't notice the many ditches which crossed the terrain below me in time. My plane overturned immediately upon hitting the ground.

It was dead quiet. I was lying head down in a ditch, that was my life saver. With great effort, I was able to keep my head above the water level. Soon I heard voices. They were Dutch, and I understood they feared that the plane might explode any minute. They went for help and after about half an hour German soldiers turned up. With a lot of effort, they pulled me from the wreck of my plane. From a stretcher, I then saw the catastrophe. Finally, I was transported to a hospital in Breda for treatment. The hot oil had burned my face

Feldwebel Werner Möszner of 9./JG 26 posing with his Me 109 G-6 in August 1943.
WERNER MÖSZNER

Feldwebel Werner Möszner is congratulated on his twenty-first birthday on August 18, 1943, by his crewchief (*Erste Wart*) *Obergefreiter* Tewes on Schiphol airfield. With flowers in his hands, he sits on his Me 109 G-6 16394 *Gelbe 12.* WERNER MÖSZNER

and upper part of my body. It took many months before I was able to fly again. However, I was then declared unfit for combat and served as instructor pilot until the war's end.

Möszner had crashed just north of Waalwijk. He is adamant that he was hit by a tail or top turret gunner. Judging from the location where he went down, this gunner belonged to the 303rd Bomb Group. Another German fighter was definitely hit by the gunners aboard the bombers. Flying in Me 109 19783 *Weisse 3* of 7./JG 26 was *Feldwebel* Wilhelm Mensing. After taking hits, his ship crashed in the Maas River near Waspik. Mensing was badly wounded and lost one of his arms as a result.

The loss of Mensing and Möszner from their formation did not stop the rest of JG 26 from their attacks on the B-17s. All too soon they scored their first success. *Hauptmann* Klaus Mietusch, the *Gruppenkommandeur* of III./JG 26 accounted for a B-17 near Raamsdonksveer just a few minutes later. Claiming a B-17 at about the same time in that same area was *Unteroffizier* Johannes Rathenow of 1./JG 1. Thus, fighters of both JG 1 and JG 26 were definitely involved in the combats with the 303rd Bomb Group. Don Gamble, pilot of B-17F 41-24562 *Sky Wolf,* wrote in his diary that night:

The wreck of *Gelbe 12* in Waalwijk after an unsuccessful belly landing. Its pilot, Werner Möszner, miraculously survived and is on a stretcher between both German soldiers on the left. WERNER MÖSZNER

Miss target on first run. We go around for another run, heading into sun. Lead plane doesn't bomb, others drop erratically, believe none hit target. Jerry fighters come in, mostly head-on. G-192, leading our squadron, gets hit. Fire starts in number three engine, spreading to number four. We fall back and he goes down to the right. Wally, my copilot sees plane explode and wing come off. We try to take over lead of squadron but other ships are low, so we fly just behind and to the left of lead ships. Enemy fighters are eager today and we see 20mm shells exploding all around. Our number four engine is hit and catches on fire. I sideslip and it goes out, but have to feather prop. 20mm explodes outside nose and knocks bombardier, Ralph Coburn, out. 20mm knocks a piece out of our rudder.

Sky Wolf's navigator was William D. McSween. He, too, kept a diary and noted that evening, still keyed up:

A "milk-run" that turned into the shakiest of all "shaky do-s." Just a short haul before supper—but we made two runs over the target— then it was "Murder Inc." Everything OK to I.P. Haze pretty bad, had to look close for check points. Had good run to target, could see aiming point plainly. Lead navigator was hit and lead bombardier did not drop bombs. Major Calhoun made circle and came over second time. Lead and high groups pulled out. P-47 cover shoved. Out of mist and haze, FW 190s struck like devils from hell. From eleven to one o'clock, diving at forty-five degrees. They made us really know it. They got three ships and shot hell out of a lot more. G-192 went down and blew up. Don saved us by a violent pull up. Number four was hit and caught fire—went out when Don slipped the plane. One third of the rudder was shot away. A 20mm burst right in the nose, blew a big hole, and knocked Coburn into my lap.

Leading the low squadron, in which *Sky Wolf* flew, was 1st Lt. James S. Nix in B-17F 42-3192, with fuselage code VK-G. Nix was a veteran pilot in the 359th Bomb Squadron on his twenty-fourth mission. He had come over with the group in October 1942 and started flying as copilot with William R. Calhoun's crew. When Calhoun was promoted to command the 359th Bomb Squadron, Nix became first pilot and now he had just one more mission to go before his tour would be over. The crew he was flying with, was a large part of the crew of 2nd Lt. Daniel A. Shebeck of the 358th Bomb Squadron. Shebeck himself flew in the copilot's seat. In addition to the ten men regularly aboard, there was a passenger along. This was the assistant engineering officer of the 359th Bomb Squadron, 1st Lt. Louis T. Moffatt.

Gelbe 12, with Waalwijk in the background. Note that the nose of the plane with the propellor has separated from the fuselage and tail. Also in the picture is the ambulance used for transporting its wounded pilot. WERNER MÖSZNER

Navigator aboard was 2nd Lt. Dwight M. Curo, who kept an extensive diary during his stay in prison camp, in which he also described the events during some of his missions. Despite the length of his account, it is almost completely recorded here because of its excellence in describing the events and feelings aboard the stricken plane.

On the eighteenth of August, we rested and on the nineteenth received an easy assignment in token of our work of two days before. This latest raid was to be a short one into Holland—a "milk run" the boys called it at briefing and so it appeared.

A quick trip over the Channel, a short distance to an airport inland, unload, and return—an easy mission. Too easy, as it turned out, for one Lt. D. M. Curo and his crew. I can't truthfully say that the mission worried me, and yet I remember a sense of forbading and presentiment, which I dismissed as nerve strain from the previous raid into Germany.

We were to fly with a split crew. Danny Shebeck, my regular pilot, was to fly with us as copilot for Lieutenant Nix, an old and experienced pilot on his twenty-fourth sweep. Spencer's place was taken by Lieutenant Solverson. Our enlisted boys were all aboard with the exception of Sergeant Tudor, radio operator, whose work was to be taken over by Sergeant Brooke from another crew; Sergeant Tudor being in the hospital with a bad foot. [First Lieutenant Charles W. Spencer was severely wounded in action on the November 26, 1943, mission to Bremen. For his actions that day, he was awarded the Distinguished Service Cross, America's second highest award for valor. Technical Sergeant M. E. Tudor was shot down and made prisoner of war on the January 11, 1944, mission to Oschersleben.] Our take-off, scheduled for 1330 hours, was delayed because of low cloud cover until almost 1630 hours. I might also add at this time the fact that we had "company" for this trip. Because of the presumed ease of the run, Lieutenant Moffatt, a ground officer of the 359th Squadron, decided to accompany us for the experience and to take a few pictures. He had obtained permission from the wing staff a few days before to make such a trip. Had he been able to foresee the events to come, I doubt that he would have been so eager "to see what a raid was like."

The clouds thinned about 1620 hours, equipment was given a last-minute check, ammunition brought up, Mae Wests and parachute harnasses adjusted, the big motors were "reved up" and off we went. Gradually circling the field, we fell into formation and with

The staff of III./JG 26 in July 1943 on Nordholz. Second from right is *Hauptmann* Klaus Mietusch, the *Gruppenkommandeur* of III./JG 26. On August 19, he claimed to have shot down a B-17 northwest of Breda at 1923 hours, for his forty-eighth combat victory. This was B-17F 42-3192 of the 303rd Bomb Group, which crashed in Raamsdonksveer. WERNER MÖSZNER

Unteroffizier Johannes Rathenow of 1./JG 1. He claimed a B-17 destroyed near Oosterhout at 1926 hours. This was B-17F 42-3192 of the 303rd Bomb Group, which was also claimed by *Hauptmann* Klaus Mietusch of JG 26.

ROB W. DE VISSER

July 1943. *Oberleutnant* Paul Schauder and *Leutnant* Gerhard Karl (killed in action on August 23, 1943) of 9./JG 26 are playing with Hasso, *der Staffelhund.* Both flew against the American bombers on August 19.
WERNER MÖSZNER

the "big ass birds" slowly lifting their heavy bomb loads higher and higher to the desired altitude we straightened out on course to the rendezvous with our lead group. The latter we met satisfactorily over Peterborough at 8,000 feet and fell in neatly below and behind them, at the same time turning to the heading for our zero point on the English coast.

At the coast outgoing, we were a minute early. I informed pilot and the crew of our time and position. Our altitude at this point was according to flight plan and so we continued our climb on course and turned out over the Channel toward the hostile coast, visible low and flat looking mid the light distant haze. It was a beautiful day for flying. The early vapors had cleared. The only evidence of clouds a few scattered fleecy ones.

The sun, getting down in the sky, shone from behind us on the waves of the Channel. A convoy passed below us off the coast looking like black specks on the gray, blue ocean carpet. The enemy coast appeared more definite in the haze, lying apparently peaceful and quiet, dead ahead. We came in over the Holland estuary, skirting the two islands lying in its mouth. From them a few sparse bursts of flak arose ahead and to the left—sensitive feelers getting our course and range. No fighters in sight. We made our turn inland.

Altitude right, airspeed right, visibility good, on course and fifteen minutes to the target—we cruised on. Gradually, the estuary narrowed beneath us, flashes from the ground, betraying the evidence of antiaircraft fire. The forming black, ugly puffs became thicker and closer ahead and to our right as we passed north of Antwerp. Up from the fields below the fighter opposition was beginning to rise in short, fast circles. At the I.P., or initial point of bomb run, the flak, though not intense was increasing and was becoming devilishly accurate. The puffs were appearing at our exact level, a few feet ahead or on either side. Occasionally, you could hear the angry burst above the roar of our motors and that is too close. A few fighters had reached our altitude and were making half hearted passes at the compact formation ahead of us. Jerry pursuits would never, except in rare cases, attack at close range a close formation of 17s— our firepower was too great. In most cases, flak would disable a plane or set it afire and the fighters would "hop" the straggler. In too many instances were they successful.

Sky Wolf and her officers. From left to right: William D. McSween (navigator), Ralph F. Coburn (bombardier), Walter R. Kyse (copilot), and Donald W. Gamble (pilot). *Sky Wolf* was lost on the mission to Oschersleben on January 11, 1944.
WILLIAM D. MCSWEEN

The target appeared ahead. As the big ships ahead of us opened their bomb bay doors, Lieutenant Solverson, opened ours and prepared to "let go" our load. The group ahead swung off course for a moment, then back. The target, plainly visible, was passing beneath us. Time to drop the bombs!!

But our lead ship appeared unsure. Bomb bays yawned, waiting to disgorge their eggs, but our formation flew serenely on, waiting for the lead group. On, on, over the target and still those ships ahead did not spew forth the expected load. What had happened? I don't know. Perhaps some day I shall, though at this writing it matters little the fault or blame. What does matter is that men died because of that mistake. The most probable conjectures are that the lead ship lost the target or that there was a malfunction in the bomb discharge mechanism. At any rate, we did not "get in and get out" as we should have.

Major Calhoun in the lead decided to make another run. Perhaps he was right. Perhaps the importance of the target did justify such an act. It is not my place to condemn or criticise. But I cannot help but feel somewhat resentful of that first abortive run and the decision to correct it. Resentful—not of my present position which is the result of that decision, but resentful of the ships and lives which were lost because of it.

Flak and fighters were, by this time, intense. As we started the big, long turn necessary to get back over the target, they had our range and how!! Flak all over and fighters in swarms. We were in for a rough time, how rough, I did not yet realize. But we were into it and there was no returning. Into that blizzard of black clouds we flew. All guns firing full power at the deadly buzzing fighters besetting us on every side. Light bursts struck the ship further back, making a short, metalic sound. No time to use the interphone for inquiries or to call out fighters. Every man firing rapidly from every position, the motors a full thrusted roar as we ploughed on.

Close to the target, we got one—a bang and crash of metal—the ship lurched on—no apparent or material damage. We were getting our share of the opposition. An Me 109 from the left, coming in and down on the squadron ahead, blew up in mid air. A dazzling burst of flame and wreckage. No chute billowed out from that one. Another diving fighter made his pass, faltered in his smooth, comet-like flight, as a thin blue stream of smoke trailed behind him and rapidly became a thick, black column plunging down.

We were still on the run. At the target, Solverson, dropped his guns and watching the lead group ahead, dropped our bombs with theirs. It was "Bombs Away!" from all the ships as the "nests of eggs" fell and the "rain" of black missiles sped earthward. At the side nose gun, Moffatt, the ground officer and our passenger, was doing noble work. He did not appear to be excited. That in itself was a load from the shoulders of Solverson and myself, who had plenty to do without worrying about an inexperienced man. We had made our turn toward home and I had just begun to think that perhaps we could "squeeze" through, when we caught a burst of flak in number four engine cell. That was the beginning of the end—there was a sharp report, the prop raced with a speed that wrecked the whole

The crew of B-17F 42-3192 of the 303rd Bomb Group, posing in July 1943 on Molesworth in front of B-17F 41-24539 *Jersey Bounce*. They were shot down by German fighters and crashed near Raamsdonksveer, Holland, on August 19. Back row, left to right: 2nd Lt. Daniel A. Shebeck (pilot, KIA), 2nd Lt. Dwight M. Curo (navigator, POW), 2nd Lt. Paul W. Campbell (copilot, not on mission), 2nd Lt. Charles W. Spencer (bombardier, flew with Lieutenant Thompson aboard *Jersey Bounce Jr*). Front row, left to right: Staff Sgt Frank F. Perez (ball turret gunner, POW), Tech Sgt. Mark E. Tudor (radio operator, not on mission), Tech Sgt. Frank G. Krajacic (engineer, KIA), Staff Sgt. Joseph Gross (left waist gunner, POW), Staff Sgt. Fred W. Boyd (tail gunner, POW), Staff Sgt. George W. Buck (right waist gunner, POW).
MARY M. MCINTYRE / FRANK F. PEREZ

ship. Sparks shot out from the motor. The prop slowed and stopped and a stream of fire reaching beyond our range of vision cascaded from the entire engine and wing surface. Fire!! The worst possible development. The old Forts came home blasted and torn by shell fire and shot to pieces by fighters. They course their rugged way through the skies, with motors out and wing surfaces disabled. Armored and powerful as they are, they are hard to bring down, but a fire aboard is a catastrophe.

"Fire in number four engine" came over the interphone from the pilots' compartment. Calmly and coolly they spoke, whether it was Nix's or Shebeck's voice, I do not know. It was the last we heard from either of the boys above us, for at that moment as I turned to grab the CO_2 extinguisher from the brackets beneath my console table, a Focke Wulf poured in on us from the right. He came from out of the sun, in a power dive straight as a speeding arrow he struck. He was well in range before he fired and he let go with the works. The leading edge of his wings seemed to belch fire as his 20mm cannon and machine guns bore down on us. Our right wing and top surface of the cockpit seemed to be consumed by tiny dancing jets of flame as he sprayed us with that deadly hail. I think that our pilot and copilot died in that rain of death. Obviously, the engineer, Sergeant Krajacic, who manned the top turret, would have prevented so close an approach by the fighter by the fire power of his twin 50s. Whether Krajacic was wounded and unable to fire or whether he was blinded by the glare of the sun is debatable. As Krajacic was a good shot with that power turret I do not believe that if the Sgt saw him or could fire, the Jerry would suddenly come in as he did for the kill.

As the fighter plane's belly flashed over us, our plane started into a smooth, though rapid, dive. The thought flashed into my mind that the pilot was diving the ship in an attempt to extinguish the blaze, which by now was consuming the entire number four engine cell, wing tip, sweeping the entire side of the ship and spreading rapidly inward toward motor number three and our wing gasoline tank.

At this moment, Moffatt, kneeling behind me tapped me on the back and motioned toward the passageway behind us. As I turned, my heart literally jumped, the entire passageway was black with turgid, rolling black smoke. Little tongues of flames leapt from amid this black mass, stabbing greedily at the gas lines and oxygen tanks, which lined the interior of the fuselage aft of the cockpit. It was a roaring, blazing inferno of flames. Objects were indistinguishable through the glare and brilliance of that terrible consuming fire. I pumped the extinguisher in its direction—a feeble effort. Smoke poured in on us. The acid smell of burning metal and leather permeated through our oxygen masks. We were afire at 20,000 feet in the air—a flaming comet of fire. Three feet behind Moffatt and in the passage was the exit hatch. To reach it appeared to be impossible through the smoke and flames now rampant in that hole behind us. Signaling to Moffatt to grasp the emergency release handle immediately behind the bulk head, I yelled over the interphone: "Danny!! (Shebeck). We're in flames down here!! Hitting the silk!!" There was no answer—my voice sounded as though I shouted into a tin can. The interphone was out. I shouted again to the crew to jump but it was obvious from the dead sound that I was talking to myself. The interphone was completely dead, shot out or destroyed by fire.

Molesworth, December 5, 1942. Lieutenant James S. Nix is proudly indicating his wife's first name, Goldie, on the number one engine cowling of B-17F 41-24581 *The 8 Ball*. This aircraft was salvaged after a belly landing fifteen days later. CHARLES R. TERRY

Moffatt's head reappeared inside the nose compartment. By frantic motions, he signalled that the emergency release handle could not pull loose. Were we trapped in the nose of that plunging fireball? I will not attempt to analyze my thoughts at that moment. They say that drowning persons envision their entire life in the moment before death. No such sensations were my lot. Fear was my only reaction, and I do mean fear. In one second, that tunnel of flame was going to reach forward into the nose and engulf us all. Those gas lines and oxygen tanks would let loose and the resulting mixture would blow us into eternity. That, believe me, is a horrible thought. But, to toast like a cinder in that wreck was not my idea of fun. Lunging forward in a sprawling dive, which snapped the oxygen mask from my face and broke the interphone connections from my helmet, I landed halfway into that passageway, my head and torso through the doorway, my legs pushing behind me. My flying helmet and flying suit protected me for the moment, and neither breathing or seeing I stabbed at the handle of the door release with

On Molesworth, Lieutenants Lumpkin, Moffatt, and Green are studying a model of a German FW 190 fighter. Moffatt was the assistant engineering officer of the 359th Bomb Squadron. He was shot down and made prisoner of war while flying as an observer on the crew of 1st Lt. James S. Nix. LOUIS T. MOFFATT

my gloved hand and jerked with all the strength of that terrible moment. The handle and the release wire gave way and raising myself slightly I came down with the heel of my hand in a solid smash on the forward edge of the door, which tore open and whisked into space with a clatter as it struck the under fuselage and tail surface. A rush of cold air followed through the opening and light came into that trap of billowing smoke and flames. How good that air was as we tore through it!

The vapors and exhaust from the left wing motors swished by. We were in the open! We had a way out! But there was no time for self congratulations. The heat and flames were still intense though swept back momentarily by the inrush of air from without. At any second, that flaming coffin in which we rode might blow sky high. And then, we started to spin. The plane suddenly whipped over on its back flinging us about like ten pins.

I grasped the edge of the exit hatch at the first lurch and hung on as the stricken bird revolved. As we came again on even keel the plane momentarily righted itself. I took a quick look behind me. Moffatt was right behind me, breathing on my neck. Solverson, behind him, had also righted himself from the gyrations and was fumbling with his chute and harness connections. He appeared to be ready to go, though rather dazed and disbelieving. I pulled myself forward through the opening, glanced to see if the bomb bay doors were open, which they were not, felt the cold blast of air beat at my upper body, and shoved off head first to avoid any possibility of hitting the plane with my head as I plunged.

I had often speculated as to my reactions at jumping with a chute: I had wondered what it would be like and if I would be hesitant or afraid to leap into space. As it happened, there was no time for fear or reactions. My feeling at leaving that plane was one of immense relief. I dove through that opening, gratefully and with no semblance of delay. I was never so glad to leave anything as I was that ship. As it happened, it was not a second too soon. The air current caught me and whisked me away from the ship. There was a sensation of utter lack of control, I was whirled and tossed over and over.

The clouds, sky, and ground became a jumble of color. The rush and noise of the air was deafening but there was no shock or sensation of falling as is felt in a short fall. Then there came a terrific noise and explosion at a distance. I could feel myself suddenly propelled through the sky and something tore at the leg of my flying suit. I searched for the rip cord handle with my right hand. My

The 303rd Bomb Group's lead crew after the July 30, 1943, mission to Kassel, posing in front of B-17F 41-24562 *Sky Wolf*. Standing are, far left, William V. Chamberlain (navigator) and, far right, Robert K. Solverson (bombardier). Kneeling second from left is George R. Redhead (waist gunner). Both Chamberlain and Redhead finished their tours on August 19 aboard *Yankee Doodle Dandy* and *Hell's Angels*, respectively. Robert Solverson was killed in the crash of B-17F 42-3192 near Raamsdonksveer that same day. Standing, still wearing his Mae West life preserver, is Lt. Col. Kermit D. Stevens. He became commanding officer of the 303rd Bomb Group six days later.
GEORGE R. REDHEAD

recollections at this point are very vivid. I remember grasping the carrying handle of the chute and by its feel of that flat webbed texture identifying it from the round, hard handle of the parachute release; the latter being partially withdrawn into, and covered by, a small canvas indentation in the chute case. Searching out the handle I grasped it firmly and pulled. There was a sudden jerk; my feet whipped downward, there was a quick pressure as of a light blow on my rump and thighs, my neck snapped backward, though not viciously and there I was a parachutist. The first noticiable thing was a vast and great silence. From the noise and hubbub which I had just experienced, it seemed a great contrast. There seemed to be no sound whatsoever. I thought for the moment that I had been deafened. Gradually, the soft singing of the parachute and it shroud lines intruded itself upon my conscience—a sight sighing. I can

remember thinking how pretty it was. Looking up I saw the big, billowing, cloth above me. It was well filled and the shroud lines ran
straight and true to the steel circular fasteners on my harness.
There came then a sense of motion and indeed I was moving; sway-
ing gently back and forth as though in a craddle. In the west the sun
was sinking, the clouds and sky above colored and beautiful in its
rays. Below me spread the countryside of Holland. The compact little fields, the rivers and the trees all outlined and vivid in their color
and their clarity. There were no planes in sight. I twisted myself to
look westward thinking that perhaps our squadron was still visible.
They were not, we had fallen far behind before our final exit.

As I turned back, the momentum swung me about. There about
a hundred yards distance at about the same height as myself was our
plane or rather its remains. It had exploded in mid air, just after I

This picture of a debriefing of a Fortress crew was published in a U.S. newspaper in
1943. Most probably, it was taken after the August 12 mission to Gelsenkirchen. In
the center is James S. Nix, wearing the white scarf around his head. Most of the
others on this picture flew aboard the 303rd Bomb Group's lead ship on August 19.
Seated on the far left is William C. Calhoun, and to the left of Nix, wearing the
flying cap, is Arnold S. Doran. Standing from left to right are Paul P. McGee,
Joseph Kerr, and Paul C. Lemann. GEORGE W. VOGEL

left it. I had felt the force of that concussion, but had cleared in time. The tail and waist were in one piece and were gliding smoothly downward. About ten yards below and slightly ahead was the nose section. It had begun to fall more rapidly and to turn. As it did so, the upper part, or turret section was completely gone, the right wing was missing and the left wing a distorted ragged piece of metal. It was still consumed by flames. No life was visible in the interior, lighted through the windows by the raging furnace within. The air was filled with small pieces of wreckage tumbling by me.

As I watched, pieces detached themselves from the wreck and floated downward. The wreck gradually disappeared below me. I took stock of myself: my nose was bleeding and my neck felt stiff and painful. There was a burning sensation below my right ear, but it was not intense and as I reached up my hands encountered a small scorched area. Evidently a result of the fire or contact with a bit of the red hot wreckage. The lower right leg surface of my flight suit was in shreds, but there was no pain or blood apparent on the member. I put it down mentally as a near miss by flak or particles from the plane explosion and once again expressed a silent but heartfelt prayer of thanks for my escape from death or serious injury.

A couple of Focke-Wulff fighters were coming up from below and heading toward me. I eyed them warily. I was a dead duck if they felt vengeful and on occasions fliers have been pierced by machine gun slugs as they dangled helplessly in their chutes. They reached my level and circled me in a wide arc; making no move or motion; they swung off and headed inland. I breathed a sigh of relief. I estimated that at this time I was about 5,000 feet up and I began to experience the sensation of descent. Signs of life began to be apparent beneath me. Off to my right and near the ground I saw a chute. As it hit, I counted two more closer to me, but below—they were about six miles distant. And then two more further out and below. Five were all I could see and looking all about me I realized that those were all and that half of my crew had perished in that fire and explosion. Up until this time I had thought that by some stroke of luck we may all have bailed out but it was apparent that this was not the case.

I looked at the wreckage still spinning beneath me and off to the left and mentally wished "Danny" a goodbye. Solverson and Nix I had known but a short time. They were fine fellows. But "Danny" Shebeck was my pilot and close friend. I had flown with him for five months. We had shared the rough and the smooth together. We had gone through the training phases, and flown an ocean together—

what I saw and knew didn't seem possible. Shebeck was a great guy. Everyone liked Danny. He had little polish or fancy ways, but at heart he was a true gentleman. He was one of the most consciencious persons I have ever known. He was a very hard working fellow and did not drink or smoke or give a damn about women; yet he was very tolerant of myself and others who on occasion overdid these vices. He lived to fly. It was his only interest and all he cared about. He was a great guy and a wonderful flyer. There's a good spot waiting for him in that squadron "off in the blue."

"Target: Germany." HMSO 1944

Again, I look earthward. Broad fields spread beneath me sparsely dotted with small groves of trees and houses. Before me and about three miles distant was a little village. Along the narrow dirt road leading from it came a small car and a good number of bicycles. From a farmhouse, built along a canal to my left, came running a group of people: men, women, kids and dogs. As I neared the ground, it seemed to approach more swiftly. In fact, it looked like I was going to get a solid thump when I hit. I flexed my legs and grasped the shroud lines. The ground came up beneath me and I hit, thump!

From the front part of the bomber, only Curo and Louis T. Moffatt managed to escape death. Bombardier Robert K. Solverson, last seen fumbling with his chute, and both pilots, Daniel A. Shebeck and James S. Nix, the latter on his next-to-last mission of his operational tour, were killed. Apart from the engineer, Tech Sgt. Frank G. Krajacic, who apparently was killed by a burst of fire from the fighters, all enlisted men managed to bail out in time.

One of them was Tech Sgt. Curtis O. Brooke, the replacement for the crew's regular radio operator. He recalls:

Tech Sgt. Curtis O. Brooke, radio operator on B-17F 42-3192 of the 303rd Bomb Group. He was made prisoner of war. CURTIS O. BROOKE

When we assembled at the aircraft before take-off, I was asked by Lieutenant Nix, our pilot, if I would grant him a personal favor by taking some moving pictures to complete his album, as he was preparing to rotate back to the States. He needed the pictures of the bombs being released, dropping and exploding. I told him that I would be only too glad to. He provided a moving picture camera that was operated by the electrical system of the aircraft.

When we got over the target, I felt the rush of air as the bomb bay doors opened and left my position at the radio preparing to take pictures from the bomb bay. When I got situated, the doors closed, so I returned to my radio position. We did not drop the bombs. A few moments later, the doors opened again, so I repeated, back to the bomb bay. Again we didn't drop, so I returned to my seat. It is my opinion that the indirect cause of the loss of the aircraft, was the command's decision to make two runs over the target, keeping us vulnerable to fighter aircraft. We were downed by a fighter making a frontal attack. Almost instantly after returning to my radio position, we felt a hard jolt through the entire aircraft. I knew we were hit because I could see fire in the right wing and I could smell an odor in my oxygen mask. So I immediately prepared to abandon ship. It was my job to aid the ball turret gunner by cranking his turret up in an emergency. On entering the waist of the ship, I saw that he needed no help. He was emerging out. Joe Gross and George Buck, the two waist gunners, were at the waist door. Gross was removing the hinge release for the door. As they kicked it out, Buck, who was in front of the door, left the plane first. As Gross got in front of the door, the right wing burned off. Gross left the plane in a ball of fire, burning his face badly. The plane went into a spin, throwing me and Frank Perez against the opposite side of the fuselage.

I managed to get hold of the bottom of the door and pulled myself out, leaving Frank behind me. As I left the ship, I was not completely conscious from the lack of oxygen, it was like a dream. I found my parachute release, it seemed my parachute slowly went up above me, which in reality was not so, because it hit me in the face and broke my nose and blackened both eyes. While descending, I was aware that a German fighter was flying straight at me. I thought he was going to shoot me, but it turned out that he veered to the side at the last moment. This happened also to other crewmembers. Later we were told by a German flyer that the fighter plane was taking pictures with his gun camera film for identification.

Anyway, as I approached the ground, I saw that I was going to land in the center of an irrigation canal on a farm, which did break my fall. I was in about waist deep water. When I stood up, I saw eight or ten civilians coming across the field. I talked with them a moment and asked one of them where I could hide and he motioned behind me. There was a German military vehicle with four or five men in it, on a road a few hundred yards from us. One of the Germans was coming across the field, so there was no way of leaving for me. He brought me back to the automobile and put my parachute in the back. He had been riding a bicycle and was to take me into town. We walked.

The left wing of B-17F 42-3192 of the 303rd Bomb Group in a meadow in the Carthuizerpolder. In the background is the O. L. Vrouwe Hemelvaart church in Raamsdonksveer. This was built in 1892 and was blown up by the Germans in 1944 before the liberation of the village. GENERAL MACZEK MUSEUM

The remnants of the bomber crashed in the Carthuizer polder, between Oosterhout and Raamsdonksveer. (The exact location was close to the watertower, which is still visible today, along the Breda-Utrecht motorway.) The seven surviving crewmembers were all quickly captured and first brought to the barracks of the military police in Raamsdonksveer. The bodies of Daniel Shebeck and Robert Solverson were found that same evening near the wreck of the aircraft. A few days later, a body was found floating in the small Donge River, and finally, a fourth body was found when the wreck was recovered by a German salvage unit. All four were buried in the Dutch Reformed Cemetery in Oosterhout. In September 1945, they were reburied in the American Military Cemetery in Margraten. Nix, Shebeck, and Krajacic are still resting here. Solverson found his final resting place in the Ono Cemetery in Salem, Wisconsin, in February 1949.

During the ordeal for Lieutenant Nix's crew, the rest of the 303rd Bomb Group's formation battled their way toward the Dutch coast, still under fierce attacks by the *Luftwaffe*. Many German fighters were claimed shot down by American gunners aboard the bombers. A small selection of their claims follows.

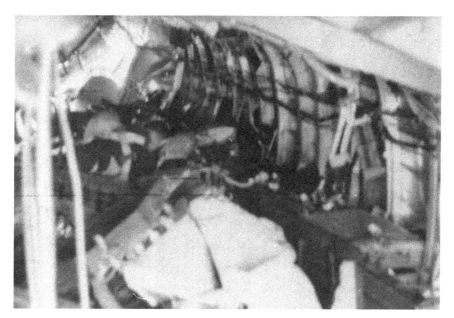

Inside the fuselage of B-17F 42-3192 of the 303rd Bomb Group after the crash.
GENERAL MACZEK MUSEUM

Sergeant Charles Warnet, ball turret gunner on B-17F 42-5257 *Miss Bea Haven*: "1810 hours, 19,000 feet, over target. FW 190 came from about two o'clock low to four o'clock. Began firing at 900 yards, came to 600 yards when his left wing fell off and he then spiralled down, burning."

Staff Sergeant Charles H. Marson, right waist gunner on B-17F 42-3029 *Wallaroo*: "1820 hours, 19,000 feet, over Dongen, Holland. Enemy fighter came in under right stabilizer from about 0430 o'clock. Right waist gunner fired about twenty-five rounds into enemy aircraft. The aircraft exploded, wings coming off and entire ship went down in flames. The aircraft was at about 350 yards when it exploded."

Staff Sergeant K. L. McGee, ball turret gunner on B-17F 42-5482 *Cat O' Nine Tails*: "1825 hours, 19,000 feet, south of Rotterdam. Had just finished fixing guns when I sighted FW 190 at 500 yards. Fired one short burst, then long burst as FW 190 came in to 400 yards. Tracers were entering between engine and cockpit. Enemy aircraft disintegrated in the air in flames."

Lieutenant James H. McConnen, navigator on B-17F 42-29664 *Jersey Bounce Jr*: "1830 hours, 18,000 feet, 4 miles east of Middelharnis. Me 109 started firing at 800 yards, came in to 300 yards continuing under ship. Hit on nose and engine and started smoking and pieces fell off. Blew up under B-17, no bail out."

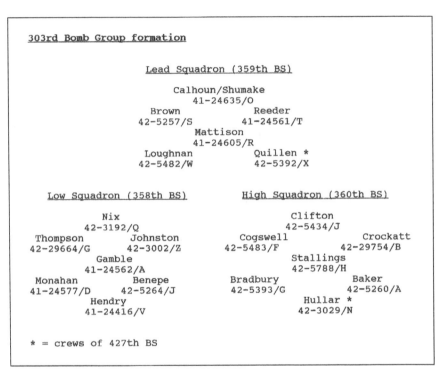

The 303rd Bomb Group formation. Shown are the names of the pilot and the serial number plus individual aircraft letter of his B-17.

Technical Sergeant Stan J. Backiel, engineer on B-17F 42-5264 *Yankee Doodle Dandy*: "1835 hours, 17,000 feet, over water. FW 190 came in about 1030 o'clock high. Opened fire at about 900 yards. Enemy aircraft came into about 300 yards, peeled off and went down in smoke. Pilot seen to bail out."

In all, the intelligence section of the First Bombardment Wing awarded twenty-one German fighters destroyed to gunners of the 303rd Bomb Group. In addition, two were confirmed damaged and one was a probable only.

As mentioned earlier, three German fighters definitely went down as a result of the gunners on this part of their route.

Me 109 20525 *Weisse 6* of 7./JG 1 was flown by *Unteroffizier* Gustav Schulze. It crashed in the North Sea, off Hook of Holland. Schulze survived. Then Me 109 *Weisse 5* of the same unit was belly landed near the village of Oud-Rozenburg by its pilot, most probably *Leutnant* Hermannes, and was only slightly damaged.

Finally, an unknown pilot was wounded in the crash of his Me 109 20521 of III./JG 1 on de Beer Island, also near Rozenburg. During the German

The crew of B-17F 42-5360 *War Bride* at Molesworth on July 20. On August 19, this crew occupied the vulnerable number-seven position in the 303rd Bomb Group's low squadron in B-17F 42-24416 *Black Diamond Express*. Standing from left to right: 2nd Lt. Calder L. Wise (copilot), 1st Lt. Jack T. Hendry (pilot), 1st Lt. Richard L. Kruse (instructor pilot, not on August 19 mission), 2nd Lt. Bernard T. McNamara (navigator), and 2nd Lt. Richard E. Webster (bombardier). Kneeling from left to right: Staff Sgt. John C. Arasin (left waist gunner), Staff Sgt John J. Doherty (right waist gunner), Tech Sgt. James J. Brown (radio operator), Staff Sgt. Olwin C. Humphries (killed in action July 30, replaced as ball-turret gunner by Sgt. Alfred J. Hargrave), Staff Sgt. Howard L. Abney (tail gunner), Tech Sgt. Loran C. Biddle (engineer). *War Bride* was lost on the mission to Oschersleben on January 11, 1944. BRIAN D. O'NEILL

fighter attacks, Sgt George W. Buske, tail gunner on B-17F 42-5264 *Yankee Doodle Dandy* flown by 1st Lt. Louis M. Benepe, went through his personal ordeal. The citation for the Silver Star medal, which he was awarded for his exploits, reads:

> For gallantry in action, while serving as tail gunner on a B-17 airplane on a bombing mission over enemy occupied Europe, August 19, 1943. Sergeant Buske's plane was subjected to repeated and

determined enemy fighter attacks. One 20mm shell penetrated the tail of the ship knocking out his left gun and exploding his tracer ammunition. Though painfully wounded, he manned his remaining gun with such skill that he destroyed one enemy plane and warded off numerous fierce attacks. The courage, skill, and devotion to duty displayed by Sergeant Buske on this occasion reflect the highest credit upon himself and the Armed Forces of the United States.

Sergeant Buske continued flying combat missions. On the December 20, 1943, mission to Bremen, he was again badly wounded at his battle station. His B-17 then had to ditch in the North Sea. For his actions aboard and the assistance rendered to Sergeant Buske in escaping from the sinking plane, the radio operator of the crew, Tech Sgt. Forrest L. Vosler, himself also wounded, was awarded the Congressional Medal of Honor.

On the same ship, bombardier Richard A. Sager and waist gunners Francis J. Stender and Edward J. Cassidy were also injured, albeit lighter than Buske. Another tail gunner was Staff Sgt. Howard L. Abney, flying in B-17F 41-24416 *Black Diamond Express*. This aircraft, flown by 1st Lt. John Hendry, occupied the vulnerable number 7 position in the low squadron. Abney went through an almost similar ordeal as Buske and recalls his story:

At our briefing, we were told this mission would be easy, a milk run; very little opposition if any would be encountered. Things didn't exactly turn out that way. It was as if we had burst open an hornets' nest. German fighter planes were all over us. As the saying goes we were well covered, but with the wrong people. I had spotted this enemy plane at a distance and recognized it as a FW 190. I had forgotten my guns were firing way left, so I had to make a great adjustment before I could do any damage to it. At last results. I had managed to hit a vital spot to set him on fire, but not enough to knock it down just then. He kept coming toward me as if to ram our plane, but he had already hit us with a 20mm explosive shell right on the spot where my ammunition was laying. This caused my ammunition to explode and I was hit by fragments in the right ankle, hip and forearm. This explosion must have rendered me unconscious, all I remember was a loud bang, as if a gun had been fired near my ear. When I came to myself, I heard a hissing sound and turned to see where it was coming from. That's when I saw a hole large enough for me to get out of the tail. Luckily for me, I knew better than to try escaping this way at 19,000 feet up. I always kept my microphone hanging at shoulder level on the right. When I tried to reach up, my right arm would not respond. I placed my

left hand on my right shoulder and started to determine what was
going on with my right arm. I pulled my arm up to inspect damages.
All I could see was a bloody mess of mangled flesh and clothing.
Even though I was severely hurt, I was still alert enough to try spot-
ting the burning plane, which I knew had not gone down. I saw it
way down in the distance, so I had enough time to leave my position
to get a member of my crew to go take my position, since I knew I
could not handle two .50-caliber machine guns with one hand. I
managed to crawl and pull myself back to the waist position. Sergeant Doherty went back to the tail. The hissing sound I had heard
in the tail was an oxygen line blown apart from the explosion of the
shells. From the waist, I made it up to the radio room and Sergeant
Brown attented to my wounds.

Just after departing the Dutch coast, near Hook of Holland and over the
North Sea, a second B-17 of the 303rd Bomb Group was mortally hit by German fighters. It was *Feldwebel* Martin Lacha of 3./JG 1 who received credit for
this kill.

Robert L. Mattison, the pilot of B-17F 41-24605 *Knock Out Dropper*, wrote
to his wife, Mary, that night:

It was to be a push-over (although I have always known that no raid
is a push-over), and off we went into the wild blue yonder, and as
the army says it, "We got our ass shot off!" Everything went haywire
and we found ourselves finally, a handful of us "in Dutch" and in a
cloud of the most persistent and deadly fighter force I'd ever been
in. I was leading the second element and I had a new pilot on my
right wing and I took the best care I could of all of us, but he was
shot down in flames right beside me, a wing-tip away. I guess God
was putting something there to shield us.

His engineer was Tech Sgt. George W. Vogel. He noted in his diary that
same evening:

The German fighters had the time to get to altitude. They attacked.
Eleven, twelve, two, three o'clock high out of the sun. They hit our
wing man. He pulled under us, number three engine burning plus
wing. I saw flames over the fuselage. They slipped under us and I
could see the gas tanks in the wing exposed. They blew up off our
left wing. As they slipped under us I could see the pilot and copilot
very clearly about thirty-five to forty feet from me. The pilot hit the
copilot on the shoulder as a sign to get out. They didn't.

Stric Nine taxiing out, numbers one and four engines running. CURTIS M. OLSEN /
ALEXANDER C. STRICKLAND

Close-up of the forward section of B-17F 42-5392 *Stric Nine.* None of the five men
flying in the forward positions on this B-17—pilot, copilot, navigator, bombardier,
and engineer—survived its demise on August 19. CURTIS M. OLSEN

This unfortunate bomber, 427th Bomb Squadron's B-17F 42-5392, nicknamed *Stric Nine*, with fuselage code GN-X, was piloted by 2nd Lt. Lauren H. Quillen and 2nd Lt. John R. Homan. It occupied the number five position in the lead squadron of the group. The crew—all but two on just their first combat mission—suffered a heavy loss of life. Tail gunner Staff Sgt. Arthur K. Sauer recalls:

> The first time I knew we were hit was when Joe Brown called the pilot: "Waist gunner to pilot: fire in number three engine." I looked back over my left shoulder and saw a small fire in number three engine. Being young and optimistic, I wasn't really concerned. I thought all the pilot had to do was to push a button to start the fire extinguisher. However, apparently the fire extinguishers had been taken out before the mission.
>
> I then understood that the plane was going to ditch, so I left my tail position. Coming to the waist, I saw Joe Brown going out, with Paul Abernathy right behind him and also the ball turret gunner leaving his position. I went back into the tail to get my parachute which was stored there and put it on. I had to pull myself out of the door, as apparently the plane was entering a spin, but got out all right. I landed furthest out, as I was the last to leave the plane, and I had to swim. My life preserver didn't work, so I went down seven or eight times. When you get under water, you get extra strength. Some boys came out in a boat, picked me up, and took me to a pier, where I was captured.

Waist gunner S/Sgt Joe H. Brown remembers the episode:

> I was the first to leave the aircraft. I landed in the water about waist deep; the others landed further out. I waded ashore carefully avoiding what I thought to be mines. All four survivors later wound up in the same lockup cold and wet. As I remember, that afternoon number three engine was feathered when the fire first started. It was in the wing between number three and four engines, the fire coming out of some air vents in the top of the wing. When the engine was restarted, the fire got big in a hurry. I believe that the flap burned into in the middle and then fell off. That was about the time that we started to get out of the airplane. Being in the back of the airplane and hooked up to oxygen and having a gun to man leaves one pretty much without knowledge of what really did happen.

2nd Lt. Lauren H.
Quillen, *Stric Nine*'s pilot.
He was killed on August
19 and was buried in the
New Eastern Cemetery
in Amsterdam on
September 1. He now
rests in Fort Morgan,
Colorado. HAZEL BENGTSON
VIA CHARLES E. HARRIS

The other waist gunner, Staff Sgt. Paul W. Abernathy, recalls:

The last thing I heard from the pilot before our communications
went dead was to prepare to ditch the plane. We were at 22,000 feet
and the flames from the burning wing were twice the length of the
plane. Several of the crew were in the waist. I told the fellows that I
wasn't going to be the first to go out, but nobody was going to beat
me for second. So the assistant engineer went out the door, and I
went right after him. I was wearing an English-type parachute, and it
didn't seem to want to open, so I had to tear it open. When it came
out, the lines hit me across the face and cut my forehead. I was floating down at about 16,000 feet and believe me, I was scared.

I looked around and I could see the coastline of Holland in the
distance. I spun around to see if I could see any other chutes. I
counted three. Then I turned back in the direction that our plane
was headed and spotted it just as the wing came off. The plane
dropped into a tailspin. The other six on board had no chance to
get out.

Now I was hanging helpless in my chute and several Me 109s
started circling me. I thought for sure that one was going to come in
on me. Now I wasn't a religious person; I had accepted the Lord
and joined the church, but didn't pray a lot. At that moment, I said,

"Lord, I'm in your hand." One of the fighters came toward me, then, all of the sudden, he banked. He flew by me, and I saw him push back his canopy, and I saw his hand come up, and he waved at me. He circled around, staying far enough away that he wouldn't mess up my chute. Then he turned and disappeared. God had heard my prayer.

My chute had a big buckle on it, like a seat belt. You would hit that thing and all the harness would fly off of you. I was prepared to push it as soon as my feet hit the water, but I wasn't quick enough, and I was pulled under for a moment. I got free and inflated my life preserver and it wasn't long before I heard a motor. The Germans had sent a boat to pick me up. When they got me on board, I was so cold and tired, it was all I could do to sit there with my hands behind my head.

Engineer Tech Sgt Eldon F. Richter. He was also killed on August 19 and was buried in the General Cemetery in Heemskerk on September 1. He now rests in Waverly, Kansas.
JOE E. RICHTER

Sauer, Brown, Abernathy, and ball turret gunner Staff Sgt. Elbert O. Price were the only ones to survive.

As Paul Abernathy already feared when floating down in his chute, the other six crewmembers of *Stric Nine* perished in or over the North Sea. The war diary of the German 719th Infantry Division, which occupied fortified positions on this part of the Dutch coast, shows, among others, the following entries:

1920 hours [German time]. Own fighter (Me 109F) crashed near combat position 63 (on De Beer Island). Crew (a *Feldwebel*) bailed out, is wounded and admitted in the hospital on the island.

1926 hours. Enemy airplane (Flying Fortress) crashed 2,000 meters south of the Brielle-Maassluis road. Five parachutes observed, drifted out of our area.

Waist gunner Staff Sgt Paul W. Abernathy was one of the four survivors of the crew.
PAUL W. ABERNATHY

The body of radio operator Staff Sgt Salvador J. DiCosmo was never recovered. His name is commemorated on the wall of the missing at the American Military Cemetery in Margraten in the Netherlands. OLIVE DICOSMO VIA SOPHIE ULJEE

Tail gunner Staff Sgt
Arthur K. Sauer also
survived and spent the
remainder of the war as
prisoner of war. SHANNON
NEAVES VIA GARY MONCUR

1937 hours. Four-engine enemy bomber crashed 6 kilometers east of Brielle on De Beer Island. From the crashed enemy planes, twelve men bailed out with parachutes. Seven of these went down in the North Sea. One "Englander" was picked up by a boat from the Maasflottila, one "Englander" was made prisoner of war by our Panzer-Jäger-Kompanie near Vlaardingen. Nothing is known about the rest. Patrols were sent out, to no avail.

1940 hours. American bomber shot down and crashed 1000 meters west of fortified position XIV (De Beer) in North Sea. Five men bailed out in sea, three of these swam ashore and were captured.

It is obvious that the last entries refer to *Stric Nine*. Its copilot, John Homan, and radio operator, Tech Sgt. Salvador J. DiCosmo, remain missing in action until the present day. Their names are inscribed on the walls of the missing at the American Military Cemetery in Margraten.

The first body that the North Sea gave back was that of pilot 2nd Lt. Lauren H. Quillen. It washed ashore on August 28 near Zandvoort. On September 1, Quillen was buried in the New Eastern Cemetery in Amsterdam. After temporary burial in Margraten immediately after the war, he now rests in Colorado.

On August 30, the body of navigator 2nd Lt. Bevan W. Colby washed up near Den Helder; he was then buried in the General Cemetery in Huisduinen. In 1946, Colby was also reburied in Margraten, where he still rests.

On August 31, engineer Tech Sgt. Eldon F. Richter's body was found near Wijk aan Zee. He was buried in Heemskerk and after the war first reburied in the American Military Cemetery Ardennes, in Neuville-en-Condroz, Belgium. He now rests in a cemetery in Kansas in the United States.

The last crewmember of *Stric Nine* to be recovered was bombardier 2nd Lt. William N. Irish. His body was found on the Scheveningen beach on September 1. Two days later, he was buried in the Westduin Cemetery in The Hague. After temporary burial after the war in the American Military Cemetery in Luxemburg, he now rests in a cemetery in Colorado.

Stric Nine had now stilled the German lust for blood. The fighters left, probably low on fuel, and the 303rd Bomb Group continued on course back to Molesworth. The nine B-17s that still had their bombs aboard jettisoned these in the North Sea.

Six crewmembers lay wounded in various ships; of them, tail gunners George Buske and Howard Abney were in bad shape. For them, the return trip probably seemed endlessly. To get the quickest medical attention for his tail gunner, 1st Lt. John W. Hendry landed *Black Diamond Express* at Framlingham. Here Abney was quickly removed from the bomber and admitted to the hospital.

Navigator 2nd Lt. Bevan W. Colby Jr. is buried in the American Military Cemetery in Margraten. AUTHOR'S COLLECTION

The main formation was back over Molesworth at 1945 hours. Their return was full of mixed emotions. On the hardstands of the two B-17s lost, there was sadness for the waiting ground crews. Only a stone's throw away there was joy: four men celebrated the end of their combat tours. Mission leader William Calhoun, navigator William Chamberlain, and gunners George Redhead and Alexander Compo were now eligible for return to the United States.

A happy warrior on Molesworth in the early evening of August 19. Having completed his twenty-fifth and final mission of his combat tour, Staff Sgt. George R. Redhead was dumped by other crewmembers into the fire pool. He had flown the mission as left waist gunner on the famous B-17F 41-24577 *Hell's Angels*.
GEORGE R. REDHEAD

The crews were debriefed by intelligence officers. Their general comments are well summarized by those of Don Gamble's crew of *Sky Wolf*: "Make only one run—let's have Spitfire escort—do not stooge off by self—have lower fighter cover—gum and candy aboard good."

The public-relations officer submitted a report for the press. He mentioned, among other things:

Single-engine enemy fighters attacked suddenly. The crews were unanimous in stating that they had never seen them come any closer.

Both Major Calhoun and Captain Shumake stated definitely that this so-called "milk run" was as tough a battle as they had ever seen.

Several crewmembers also recorded their experiences in their diaries. Engineer George Vogel, who had flown his twenty-third mission, wrote that "This was the roughest raid I've been on so far." Navigator William McSween, on his eleventh mission, wrote: "We were damn lucky to get back. Moral: one run over the target is plenty, especially if the second run is by your 'lonesome'."

Finally, pilot Robert Mattison, who had seen *Stric Nine* shot down just off his right wing, wrote to his wife:

> My other wingman and his copilot almost threw their arms around me when we landed. They were so frightened, and so grateful that I took the evasive action that saved us. It almost brought tears to my eyes. I can't tell you what this business is like—I wonder that I shall ever be able to tell you.
>
> Such things I've seen—I wonder sometimes a few hours after a session like this one if that could have been a motion picture, but even Hollywood couldn't "overdraw" so heavily.

After the mission, tension could be relieved in the various bars on the bases. This is the officers club on Ridgewell, home of the 381st Bomb Group. EVERETT F. MALONE

CHAPTER 6

Havoc in Hulten

Gilze-Rijen airfield is located between the two small villages giving it its name. However, in the northeastern corner of the airfield along the Breda-Tilburg main road lies a third, even smaller, village: Hulten. Together with the rural area around it, Hulten had some 650 inhabitants in 1940. This tiny village would be at the receiving end of many of the American bombs on August 19, 1943.

For a Dutch eyewitness account of the events, we will first look at the war diary of nineteen-year-old Jan van den Hout, living a little south of the airfield.

> In the morning, a Junkers 88 took off, flying over our heads. In the afternoon, a couple of Dornier 217s, Messerschmitt 110s, and Junkers 88s were flying around. One Junkers 52 landed.
>
> At around 1600 hours fifteen to twenty Me 109Fs landed, coming in over Hulten, they took off again at 1845 hours, heading west. [Unknown to Jan, these Me 109s belonged to JG 1 and were ordered to intercept the incoming American bombers over the Belgian coast. During the combats with escorting Spitfires, a number of these Me 109s were shot down, as described in the chapter about Flushing.]
>
> Around 1900 hours, a heavy bombing takes place, direction west-southwest. The air raid alarm sounds a few minutes later.
>
> From the southwest, a large formation of American bombers approaches, comprising of some twenty four-engine bombers, type Boeing B-17 Flying Fortress. The planes take up a course directly to the airfield, while under attack by German fighters. The heavy flak starts to fire, but can't reach the formation at its altitude. As the formation flies over the airfield, a large number of bombs are dropped (high explosives and incendiaries). These struck some hangars and farms in Hulten. Three farms were set afire. A number of deaths are reported. The bombers make a wide circle to the right and approach again, about five minutes later, from the south. Again a

151

number of bombs is dropped; now they fall in Klein Tilburg and on
hangars near Hulten. Two of the latter are burned down. Now the
German fighters start very fierce attacks. Groups of three or four
fighters attack the formation from behind and fire hundredths of little shells between the bombers. The bombers fire continuously back.
This heavy fighting goes on for several minutes. Over Oosterhout, a
B-17 is hit, flying in the middle of the group. Trailing smoke and with
a burning engine on the right wing, the plane turns to the right, losing a lot of height. Suddenly, large flames envelop the entire plane
and three Me 109s now attack the plane from short range, while
crewmembers jump out with their parachutes, five in all.

The plane goes into a spin, breaks into pieces, which gradually
float to earth. One of the wings stays in the air for a long time. On
the ground, behind Oosterhout, the remains burned for some time.

About half an hour later heavy bomb explosions can be heard
in a westerly direction. A few moments later, two bomber formations approach from the south, one formation with twenty-one
planes, the other with nineteen. They fly straight over the airfield
and are being fired upon by the heavy flak. The shells burst too
low again. No bombs are dropped this time. Scattered German
fighters fly around, but do not seriously attack the bombers. These

A huge column of smoke
rises from the hangar on
Gilze-Rijen airfield that
was hit by American
bombs. Together with it,
a Messerschmitt 110 night-
fighter was destroyed.
WOUT VAN DEN HOUT

disappear to the north-west. During the attacks, a FW 190 has landed on the airfield, probably with engine trouble. It is not unlikely that we also have seen some Allied fighters. At 2300 hours the farms are still on fire.

It is obvious that Jan van den Hout was a good observer of all aerial events and that he, as so many of his contemporaries in those days, was an avid aircraft recognizer. The B-17 whose final moments he witnessed was James Nix's B-17 of the 303rd Bomb Group.

However, where Jan only briefly refers to the damage and misery on the ground, this is not the case in the account of Koos Anssems. He was working in the fields to the north of the airfield. His story clearly reflects the horrors through which the ordinary civilians had to go in these hours and the heavy impact of the bombing on the small Hulten community.

In the late afternoon of Thursday, August 19, 1943, we were harvesting oats on our field in "het Broek." My three sisters and four of my brothers were all helping. When we left house early in the afternoon, my mother had said to us: "Whenever something happens, I will go into the cellar, you will be safe in 'het Broek'!"

Around 1830 hours, we heard the alarms for the flak gun crews at the airfields and shortly thereafter the air raid alarm sounded. We continued our work, we had experienced that so often, without something serious happening afterwards. Besides, we felt safe, comparatively far away from the airfield.

At around 1900 hours, we hear engine noises in the south and indeed, some formations of planes approach from that direction, flying very high. We can hardly distinguish them, little silver dots in the hazy sky, now and then glittering in the sun. They must be English or American, as the flak starts to fire. Then we hear bombs exploding and we can see the column of smoke and dust approach us! I can just see how the railway line is hit, when wood and iron fly through the air. We are several hundred meters from the railway line. Only seconds later, I just made it to a ditch, when all around us the bombs explode, with deafening roar . . .

All daylight has gone in the cloud of dust and nothing can be seen. "I'm hit," I hear. It is the voice of Janus, my oldest brother, who hesitated briefly before diving for cover. Immediately I jump from the ditch, but can't find my brother because of the dust. At almost the same moment, I am hit by shrapnel from the bombs, still falling. I fall down, dazed.

Hulten under the bombs as seen from 21,000 feet by the camera aboard B-17F 42-29963 of the 379th Bomb Group. In the lefthand bottom corner is the northeast corner of the Gilze Rijen airfield and, running just north of it, the Breda-Tilburg main road. A little farther north are the railroad tracks and, at the top of the picture, the Wilhelmina canal. PUBLIC RECORD OFFICE

Janus is found, badly injured, with one of his feet off. Father Joosten immediately administers the supreme unction. On the way to the Saint Elisabeth hospital in Tilburg, Janus dies in the car.

As soon as I recovered from the deafening explosions, I found out that I was hit in at least four places, neck, arm, chest, and back. But, I still can get up and, with all my strength, move. At my own strength, I manage to reach the farm of Toon van Hoek, almost hundred meters away in "het Broek." Here I get a drink, as I am very thirsty. A little later a bus arrives here, in which my wounded sisters Jo, Nel, and Ad already are. In the hospital they have to amputate one of Ad's legs. Among the others in the bus are the wife of Jan van Dongen (Cornelia de Bont, who is dead already) and four or five dead children. Near café Stad Parijs, the bus stops to take a Dutch collaborator aboard. He had been standing guard near a German searchlight and is already dying. The servant of Jan van Zon, Bart van Dun, and the little daughter of Goof Akkermans, she has lost a foot and will die in the hospital, are also brought aboard.

Then the body of the wife of Goof Akkermans, which already had been brought to the shed near Stad Parijs, is taken aboard. I get off the bus, determined to go home. But they make me get in again and I go to the hospital.

At around 2000 hours, the bus arrives at the Tilburg hospital, where everybody is assembled in one room, together with some sick German soldiers. Shortly after our arrival the apparently not very badly hurt Kees Broeders dies. [Broeders was an employee of the Dutch railway company. A memorial plaque with his name hangs in the hall of the present-day Gilze-Rijen railway station.] When the bombs fell he was busy harvesting grain, pitching it up on a cart, on which his son Leo was standing. Leo died instantly when the bombs burst close by. The horse was killed too. In a train, which passed by when everything happened, more victims fell. They were brought to Breda.

Two of the civilian victims: Cornelia Faes and Adrianus Anssems. WOUT VAN DEN HOUT

In the hospital, I am not attended to before ten minutes to two in the night. The more badly injured have occupied all doctors and nurses until that time. I have to stay in the hospital for twelve weeks and it is only due to my strict refusals that my left arm is not amputated by the doctors.

In all, twenty-three Dutch civilians lost their lives, in and around Hulten, as a result of the bombs.

The Dutch collaborator, who is mentioned in Koos Anssems's account, was Henricus Aarts. He was a so-called *Wachtmann*, standing guard near a German searchlight. This was only occupied by its crew during the nightly hours and therefore had to be guarded against sabotage during the day.

At the exact moment that the first bombs were dropped, a train, coming from Tilburg, was passing on the railway line. Shortly before the bombs hit, it stopped and the passengers dove for cover in the ditch next to the railway line. Eight passengers were injured, four of them slightly and four severely. One passenger was killed by a bomb fragment. He was twenty-five-year-old Kees Quak, a Dutch military policeman, on his way home for leave. He was buried in his home-town Rozenburg on August 24.

Deel van de lijkstoet, op weg vanuit richting "Stad Parijs" naar de Hultense kerk.
- Maandagochtend 23 augustus 1943 om ± 10.00 uur. -

The funeral of some of the civilian victims, as witnessed by Wout van den Hout in the early morning of August 23. WOUT VAN DEN HOUT

One German soldier also lost his life under the bombs. In the Protestant Cemetery Zuijlen in Breda, the body of *Leutnant* Gerhard Meyer was buried. The cemetery register records that he belonged to the 4th Battery of Light Flak Battery 847, that he was born on June 1, 1914, and died on August 19, 1943, in Gilze. The German archives do not list the exact cause of his death, but it seems very likely that he was a victim of the American bombs. Where Meyer was hit exactly is not known, but it is probable that he was killed when the second load of bombs exploded near Klein Tilburg, where an 88mm Flak gun battery was protected by a number of light 20mm cannons. After the war, Meyer was reburied in the German Military Cemetery in Ysselsteyn, the Netherlands.

Besides all the human suffering, of course, there was a great deal of other damage. Records give detailed information about lost property and livestock of the farmers in Hulten. Four farmhouses were totally destroyed, those of the families C. P. Michielsen, C. A. van Dongen, A. van Zon, and C. van Zon. One farm, a twin private house, and a cafe were badly damaged. Five farms, a private house, and another cafe were slightly damaged. Records even indicate that at least seven horses, five cows, six calfs, fourteen pigs, and three sheep were lost in the bombing.

Innocent victims of the attack. In the tiny cemetery in Rijen, the grave of the Akkermans family clearly illustrates the cruelty of war. Twelve-year-old boy Johannes was killed by the bombs on the nineteenth; his mother died of her wounds on the next day; six-year-old Maria succumbed on the twenty-first. AUTHOR'S COLLECTION

CHAPTER 7

Woensdrecht

The attacking force for the airfield at Woensdrecht was put up by the groups of the Fourth Bombardment Wing. Due to the number of bombers and their crews still in North Africa, after the shuttle mission of two days earlier, only two group formations could be mustered. Both were to be composite groups and a large number of participating crews was fairly new in the war theater.

The lead group was led by a squadron of eight bombers furnished by the 96th Bomb Group from Snetterton Heath. The seven ships in the low squadron belonged to the 388th Bomb Group from Knettishall and the high squadron was composed of a mere three bombers of the 94th Bomb Group from Bury St. Edmunds and an additional six of the 385th Bomb Group from Great Ashfield.

The second and only other group formation was composed of three squadrons from three different bomb groups. Leading the group were seven ships of the 100th Bomb Group from Thorpe Abbotts, the high squadron were seven ships of the 390th Bomb Group from Framlingham, and flying in the low squadron were seven bombers of the 95th Bomb Group from Horham.

Leading this 403rd Combat Wing was Col. Archie J. Old, the commanding officer of the 96th Bomb Group. He was flying in B-17F 42-30412 *Mischief Maker II*, piloted by Capt. Vernon L. Iverson. The story behind Old flying with Iverson on the Woensdrecht mission has a more or less comical prelude. Old had expected to lead the entire combat force to Regensburg two days earlier. However, at the last possible moment before take-off, Col. Curtis LeMay, the commanding officer of the 4th Bomb Wing, showed up at Old's aircraft and bumped him out of his expected command. Old, furious but not wanting to be left behind on this epic mission, moved his gear to Iverson's aircraft and boarded it. However, Old was not going to make it to Regensburg, as Iverson had to abort going in over the Dutch coast. Flamboyant Old, already in a bad temper after his forced move, was said to have nearly exploded upon return to Snetterton Heath. But apparently he didn't take it out on Iverson too hard, as two days later he was to fly with him again, this time to Woensdrecht.

The officers of the lead crew for the 403rd Combat Wing are pictured in front of their lead ship, B-17F 42-30412 *Mischief Maker II* of the 96th Bomb Group. From left to right: 1st Lt. Michael A. Arpaia (bombardier), Capt. Vernon L. Iverson (pilot), 1st Lt. Richard L. Davisson (navigator), and Flight Off. John L. Gawley (copilot). Standing on the right is Col. James L. Travis, who flew on August 19 as an observer aboard *Black Heart Jr* and had to bail out of the burning bomber over England. *Mischief Maker II* was lost on a mission to Berlin on March 4, 1944. VERNON L. IVERSON

Their bomber left the runway of Snetterton Heath at 1615 hours and climbed steadily to 6,000 feet to form the first composite group.

The assembly of the wing was smooth in respect to that of the Gilze-Rijen bound forces. However, one bomber of the 96th Bomb Group was lost, even before the English coast was left.

Second Lieutenant James A. Attaway and 2nd Lt. Matthew L. Vinson were flying in B-17F 42-30172 *Black Heart Jr.* Attaway and his crew had, like Iverson, aborted the Regensburg mission two days earlier. Vinson recalls that after some hours of flying on that mission the oxygen pressure had dropped to 50 percent. They returned to Snetterton Heath, where efforts were fruitless to find the cause of the oxygen loss. This was now to prove almost fatal.

Second Lt. James A. Attaway in the pilot's seat of B-17F 42-29766 *Black Heart* of the 96th Bomb Group. MATTHEW L. VINSON

Second Lt. Matthew L. Vinson in the copilot's seat of B-17F 42-29766 *Black Heart* of the 96th Bomb Group. This aircraft was scrapped because of extensive battle damage after the June 13 mission to Kiel. Vinson belly-landed its successor, *Black Heart Jr,* on fire at Wolverton Sands on August 19. MATTHEW L. VINSON

With Attaway's crew rode Col. James E. Travis, the executive officer of the 403rd Provisional Combat Wing.

James Attaway recalls the events aboard *Black Heart Jr.*

We were at 13,000 feet and climbing to altitude. The first indication of any problem was a loud explosion, followed by fire in the cockpit with heavy smoke making control of the aircraft difficult. A crewmember yelled over the intercom that we were about to collide with another aircraft on our right. With luck this was avoided and we were able to level off and ease our way out of the formation. We then determined that the oxygen system had ruptured. The oxygen was mixing with oil on the floor, leaking from the top turret, resulting in spontaneous combustion. The bomb-bay door was welded shut from the heat. The explosion caused a hole in the copilot's windshield and right side window. The navigator and bombardier reported that there was a hole in the plexiglass nose and that part of the oxygen bottle system located on the right side of the aircraft between the pilot compartment and nose section had exploded, leaving a large hole in the side of the aircraft.

At this point, with no control over the fire, the order to bail out was given. The engineer, who had been fighting the fire, went down the catwalk to bail out. I had advised my copilot, Matthew Vinson, to control the aircraft previously and I was out of my seat helping the engineer try to put out the fire. I continued to attempt to extinguish the fire without success. Vinson put the aircraft on auto-pilot and we both went down to the nose to bail out. Our parachutes had been stored near the hatch. I put my hand on one and proceeded to the nose for room to hook it on. Just prior to jumping, I saw the bombardier. I said, "Let's get the hell out of here." He answered: "I'm on my way, go ahead, I'll be right behind you." In the meantime, seeing no one else and thinking that Matthew Vinson was already gone, I bailed out.

In the rear of the plane, everybody had left the ship safely.

The next day, radio operator Sgt. Robert P. Woods wrote in his diary:

I smelled and saw smoke coming into the radio room, then heard the bail-out bell. Grabbed and hooked on my chest chute and headed for back door. Stopped to see that Moore got out of the ball turret, then on back to help Kangles to get the escape door off. Looked like it wasn't coming out, so I bailed out the right waist window. Had to use both hands to pull cord and got quite a jerk when chute opened. It didn't seem long getting down and I landed flat on my back. A jeep from a nearby gunnery school picked me up and we went about two miles away and picked up Trujillo who landed in a duck pond. Huff landed in the water not far from the beach. Garrow in the woods fracturing two ribs going down through the trees.

Copilot Matthew Vinson, however, had not left *Black Heart Jr* as Attaway had assumed. He had a very hair-raising experience. The parachutes for the pilot, copilot, and engineer were stored near the hatchway leading to the

Posing on Snetterton Heath in front of B-17F 42-30854 *Black Heart III* to celebrate its pilot's last mission is the crew of James A. Attaway. Several were involved in the August 19 incident with *Black Heart Jr*. Front row, left to right: Capt. James A. Attaway (pilot), 2nd Lt. Bertram Ripley (copilot, not on mission), 1st Lt. Alvin Jorgenson (navigator, not on mission), 1st Lt. John R. Miller (bombardier), and Matthew L. Vinson (copilot). Back row, left to right: Tech Sgt. Pete Moore (engineer, not on mission), Staff Sgt. Ed Dolan (tail gunner, not on mission), Staff Sgt. John A. Kangles (left waist gunner), Tech Sgt. Robert P. Woods (radio operator), Staff Sgt. Richard D. Garrow (right waist gunner), and Staff Sgt. William McGill (ball-turret gunner, not on mission). *Black Heart III* was lost on a mission to Bremen on November 26, 1943. MATTHEW L. VINSON

nose. When Vinson got there, he discovered that one of the explosions had blown one of these chutes out of the aircraft. Then, by accident, the top turret gunner had grabbed Vinson's chute, so he was left with no chute at all, in the burning bomber. Vinson's story starts just after Attaway bailed out:

John Miller, our bombardier, was last to leave. We were staring at each other at the forward hatch and I realized he knew I didn't have a pack. He made signs to signify that perhaps we could hook our chute harnasses together and go down in one. I knew we could not exit the hatch in that way so I grabbed his jacket and pushed him to the hatch. I had a thought that I might jump and avoid the inevitable explosion, had second thoughts, climbed into my regular seat, tried the controls and resigned myself to fly until it blew. The ship flew in wide circles, as it came into almost landing height and was parallel to the beach. It was low tide and where I landed was mud, perfect for my needs. I stalled the plane in, tail first and the belly settled down and slid to a halt. The thing was completely afire, I crawled out of the side window and tried to run. I fell and at about that time a British workman at a gunnery school picked me up and carried me into a parked ammo carrier. At the moment we started off, the plane blew.

Vinson had belly-landed *Black Heart Jr* at Wolferton Sands, on the border of The Wash, a little north of King's Lynn. He had escaped with some burns to his hands and face. For his coolness and extraordinary flying skills, he was subsequently awarded the Distinguished Flying Cross. The story made headlines in many U.S. papers.

Lieutenant Charles O. Noderer, the navigator, had trouble with his parachute on the way down. He landed extra hard and suffered some internal injuries. Left waist gunner Staff Sgt. Richard D. Garrow had a possible fracture of two ribs after crashing through some trees. All three wounded were admitted to the same hospital. The rest of the crew was safe and sound. (Despite this bad start for Colonel Travis with the 96th Bomb Group, he was appointed as its commanding officer on September 6, 1943, and remained until June 1944.)

In the meantime, both groups in the wing had formed up and left the English coast one minute behind schedule at 1813 hours. Lead navigator 1st Lt. Richard L. Davisson, aboard *Mischief Maker II*, somehow took the groups off the briefed track and drifted eleven miles off course to the south. The formation now entered the enemy coast three miles north of Blanken-

The skeleton of B-17F 42-30172 *Black Heart Jr* after it exploded on the beach near Wolverton. GEOFFREY D. WARD / ROBERT E. DOHERTY

berghe in Belgium. Davisson immediately corrected his course and arrived at the scheduled initial point at 1844 hours. In the meantime, a complete cloud cover had added to Davisson's problems.

In the vicinity of the initial point, the clouds broke, but in turn, a heavy ground haze produced extremely low visibility in the target area. However, all aircraft in the formation opened their bomb-bay doors for the bombing run on Woensdrecht airfield. Because of the restricted visibility and the strict orders not to bomb indiscriminately, the bombs were not dropped on the first run. Instead of making a second run on Woensdrecht, the wing set course for the assigned secondary target, Gilze-Rijen, with the bomb bay doors still open. Here they arrived at 1855 hours, but again ground haze hampered visibility and combat wing commander Colonel Old decided to head back to England without dropping his bombs at all. This was the formation that the scared civilians in Hulten, among others Koos Anssems, had seen approaching some time after they had been hit by the bombs of the 103rd Combat Wing. Old then decided to try to hit Haamstede airfield, on the tip of Schouwen Island, on the way back. Here again weather prevented any bombing.

When the formation was approaching Gilze-Rijen, it was fired upon by the 2nd and 3rd Batteries of Mixed Flak Battalion 665, which had their positions close to the airfield.

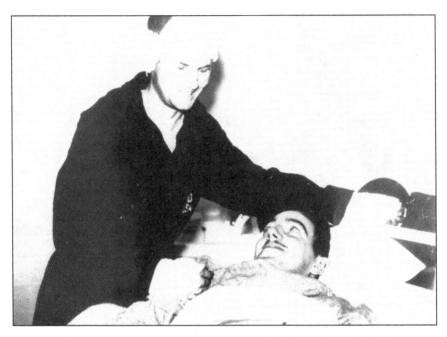

The day after. Bandaged Matthew L. Vinson visits the bed side of Charles O.
Noderer, who was injured in his parachute jump. MATTHEW L. VINSON

Oberleutnant Schutte, commanding the 3rd Battery, reported:

On August 19, 1943, we were at battle stations since 1847 hours
(German time). At 1955 hours, after we had already fired on two
other formations, a new formation of American bombers,
approaching the airfield from four o'clock, was picked up. At 1959
hours, fire was opened on the formation, which flew at an altitude
of 6,500 meters, at extreme range of almost 9.5 kilometers.

According to observers, our salvos were well aimed and evasive
action and unrest in the formation could be noticed. At the end of
our firing a definite smoke trail, gradually increasing, could be seen
coming from one of the airplanes. At 2001 hours, we stopped firing,
after using seventy-six rounds of 88mm ammunition. The bomber
formation continued on course, flying from four to ten o'clock.
However, the stricken bomber with the smoke trail had left the formation shortly after being hit, and turned to the left, in the direction of nine o'clock.

The bomber that was hit and had left the formation was B-17F 42-30068
of the 388th Bomb Group, 561st Bomb Squadron. It was flown by the crew

of 2nd Lt. Benjamin Howe Jr., on their third combat mission. They were briefed to fly in the number 7 position in the low squadron. After *Black Heart Jr* of the 96th Bomb Group dropped out of the formation over England, a vacancy in the lead squadron presented itself, and Howe and his crew moved up and occupied it. No doubt, they felt it was safer in the lead squadron. It turned out to be a very fateful decision. The 388th Bomb Group's Intelligence section reported that evening:

> Howe's ship was the only ship lost over enemy territory by the Wing on this mission. Apparently, his ship was struck by flak either over Ostend or more probably over the primary target. His number four engine caught fire, and he dropped out of formation. According to reports, his ship was able to extinguish the fire and to feather the number four prop. When the wing formation swung inland to go to the vicinity of the secondary target and then came back to the rally point, Howe was able to get back into formation by cutting the turn short, and is reported to have fallen in with the second group. About the vicinity of the rally point, the second group speeded up a bit to close the gap between the first and second groups, and apparently, the pace here was too much for Howe. He then dropped out

Colonel Archie J. Old has just presented the Distinguished Flying Cross to Matthew L. Vinson and is now pinning one on Warren F. Bacon. The latter piloted *Dry Run III* and barely missed a collision with *Black Heart Jr* over England on August 19. Old himself flew as combat wing commander in *Mischief Maker II* that day.

of formation and made for the deck. The ship is reported to have jettisoned its bombs. He was last seen at a very low altitude silhouetted against some clouds just off the Dutch coast at Haamstede. At this point his plane was completely under control, but two crews reported seeing several fighters attack him. They apparently went down in the Channel somewhere between Haamstede and Felixstowe. Air-Sea Rescue sent out a distress signal on the international frequency, so both English and Germans instituted searches. If he was able to ditch successfully there was a considerable chance that he was picked up by the enemy.

Unfortunately, this was not to be. As the other 388th Bomb Group crews already had noticed, the bomber was intercepted by several FW 190s between the target and the coast. These fighters belonged to JG 1 and JG 26 and had most probably already been in action against the 103rd Combat Wing near Gilze-Rijen shortly before.

Howe then took his bomber down to make the approach for the enemy fighters more difficult. Several inconclusive passes were made by the FW 190s. The coast and North Sea were near when Howe had the bad luck that his course led him, at this low altitude, over two German light flak batteries at the western edge of Schouwen Island, northwest of the village of Haamstede. These flak batteries were part of the German coastal defense system along the North Sea.

The commanding officer of the 3rd Battery of Light Flak Battalion 847 reported:

On August 19, 1943, at 2010 hours (German time), after earlier warnings of returning bombers, we heard engine noises coming from three o'clock. A single four-engine plane of the Fortress II type, was seen coming out of the clouds at 1,600 meters. It slowly lost altitude and was fired upon by my Vth and IVth platoons, at a distance of respectively 1,200 and 1,400 meters and a height of 1,000 meters. All available guns were firing. Shortly after opening fire, eyewitnesses reported strikes on the target. The plane then started smoking, and a few seconds later flames were seen. After our fire, a number of crewmembers jumped out. Two parachutes opened itself and could be seen for some time. In all, we fired 210 rounds of high-explosive tracer and 45 rounds of high-explosive/ incendiary tracer ammunition.

Both the members of the battery and other eyewitnesses noticed hits in the fuselage, which first caused smoke and then fire. The plane then lost more height, losing several smaller parts, then went down over its left wing, which broke off, and went straight into the ground, one kilometer east of the airfield.

One of the German eyewitnesses was *Unteroffizier* Gunter Hanke, who reported:

Yesterday evening at around 2000 hours, I was near the administrative building on Haamstede airfield. A few minutes past eight o'clock, I saw a big four-engine bomber approaching the airfield from the northeast. Its left wing was clearly damaged. Then the flak opened fire on the plane. I could clearly see how the first burst closely went past the plane, while the second burst hit the bomber, in the middle and a little to the front. Immediately, I noticed that the plane started smoking and a dark smoke trail appeared. A few seconds later, I also noticed flames. The burning plane lost a lot of height, then crashed. Thick black smoke rose from the ground. Shortly after the opening of fire by the flak, I noticed that a man left the plane with a parachute. I had the impression that the bomber was damaged by fighters, but that the flak hits gave the final blow. I could clearly see the hits, because they fired tracer ammunition.

Aboard the B-17, havoc was created by the deadly slugs. Somehow, Benjamin Howe managed to ring the bail-out bell, for those of his crew still alive after the hail of German fire.

Bombardier was 2nd Lt. Joel H. Tutt, who recalled:

The last contact with most crewmembers was on interphone for a last oxygen check, just before the fighters hit us.

The bail-out alarm sounded as we were flying over Schouwen Island, Holland. The navigator, Lieutenant Pilley, bailed out the nose hatch just before the plane went into a steep bank. I met the copilot, Lieutenant Gruhn, as I was making my way to the hatchway about the same time the plane went into the steep bank. I don't remember exactly how I got out as the force of the plane made it practically impossible to move. The next thing I remember I was in the air and on the ground about 1,500 yards from the plane. The plane landed near German quarters. I wanted to go to the plane and see about the ones that were still in, but the guards that had me would not let me.

The crew of B-17F 42-30068 of the 388th Bomb Group posing during training at Walla Walla Army Air Force Base, Washington, in late May or early June 1943. They were shot down by flak and crashed near Haamstede, Holland, on August 19. Back row, left to right: 2nd Lt. Benjamin Howe Jr. (pilot, KIA), 2nd Lt. Paul R. Gruhn (copilot, KIA), 2nd Lt. Arthur G. Pilley (navigator, POW), 2nd Lt. Joel H. Tutt (bombardier, POW), Staff Sgt. William G. Ryan (tail gunner, KIA). Front row, left to right: Staff Sgt Rardin (engineer, not on mission, replaced by Staff Sgt. James E. Hillier, KIA), Staff Sgt. George E. Connelly (waist gunner, KIA), Staff Sgt. Dale T. Butt (ball-turret gunner, KIA), Staff Sgt. William J. Stamp (waist gunner, KIA), and Staff Sgt. Stephen A. Toth (radio operator, KIA). B-17F 42-3388 was flown over the Atlantic Ocean by Howe's crew but was finally assigned to the 385th Bomb Group after arrival in England. It was ditched in the Channel on April 24, 1944, returning from Friedrichshafen. JOEL H. TUTT

In all probability, Lieutenant Gruhn helped me out, and the increasing force of the spinning plane and the lack of time prevented him from getting out.

Arthur G. Pilley, the navigator, who was first out, recalled:

Five minutes before I bailed out, Lieutenant Howe said he would try to stay in the clouds and get home that way.

My supposition is that Lieutenant Howe may have been wounded by machine-gun fire from the FW 190s. Even before we went overseas, he said he would never bail out. He may have tried to crash

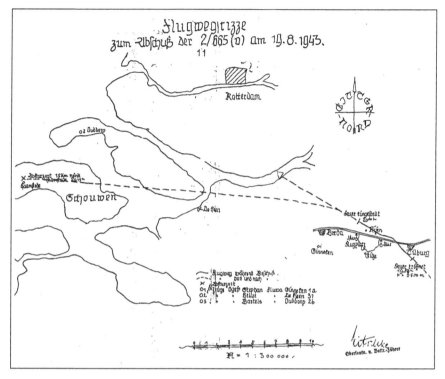

The last flight of Lieutenant Howe and his crew. This map, coming from the combat report of the 2nd Battery of *Gemischte-Flak-Abteilung 665*, shows that the battery opened fire at 1958 hours (German time) and stopped firing at 2000 hours. Shortly after that time, the bomber was seen to leave the main formation. It finally crashed at 2015 hours, just north of Haamstede. BUNDESARCHIV

land the ship; however, when I bailed out, the plane was in a steep bank to the right and diving earthward.

I met Lieutenant Gruhn in the nose hatchway, ready to bail out. He was not wounded, but his face was very flushed when I last saw him. Why he did not get out is a mystery to me; however, he may have gone back to the pilot's compartment and tried to get control of the plane so as to crash land it. When the plane went into a steep bank, the force may have glued him to the floor, making it impossible to get out the hatch. The plane crashed approximately twenty seconds after my chute opened.

It is obvious that where Tutt and Pilley mention the German fighters which gave them the coup de grace, it was the light flak which eventually brought their bomber down.

Only Tutt and Pilley in the nose of the ship survived. The eight other crewmembers, all farther back in the plane, perished in or near the wreck of their bomber. Copilot Gruhn was found by the Germans about 100 meters from the plane. Apparently, he bailed out at too low an altitude for his chute to open properly.

All eight killed crewmembers were buried in the Haamstede Military Cemetery already the next morning. Meanwhile, the German flak units were arguing who had shot the bomber down. Also no fewer than three fighter pilots submitted a claim for the destruction of a B-17 in the general area. *Unteroffizier* Bernhard Kunze of 1./JG 1 claimed a B-17 near Haamstede at 1943 hours, and both *Unteroffizier* Rudolf Hübl of 1./JG 1 and Erich Schwarz of 8./JG 26 claimed a B-17 at 2000 hours over Brouwershaven and Haamstede respectively. Since we know that only Howe's bomber crashed at around that time in that area it is obvious these three Germans belonged to the fighters that were observed by the American crews to attack Howe's straggling Fort.

Boise, Idaho, early 1943. The crew of Lieutenant Howe of the 388th Bomb Group in the early stage of crew assembly, still without a copilot and a navigator. In front is pilot Benjamin Howe Jr. Kneeling, from left to right: tailgunner William G. Ryan, engineer Rardin, bombardier Joel H. Tutt, ball-turret gunner Dale T. Butt, and waist gunner George E. Connelly. Standing on the left is waist gunner William J. Stamp, and on the right is radio operator Stephen A. Toth. All except Rardin and Tutt were killed on August 19. JOEL H. TUTT

Finally, the German credit board established that the victory was shared by both the 2nd and 3rd Battery of Mixed Flak Battalion 665 near Gilze-Rijen and the 3rd Battery of Light Flak Battalion 847 near Haamstede. There was no more mentioning of contributing fighters.

After the war, the mortal remains of the killed crewmembers were temporarily reinterred in the American Military Cemetery in Neuville-en-Condroz, Belgium. Four of the crew, pilot Howe, engineer Staff Sgt. James E. Hillier, radio operator Staff Sgt. Stephen A. Toth, and tail gunner Staff Sgt. William G. Ryan now rest in a group burial in the Long Island National Cemetery in Farmingdale, New York.

Waist gunner Staff Sgt. William J. Stamp is also buried in New York. The other waist gunner, Staff Sgt. George E. Connelly, rests in a cemetery in Pennsylvania. Both copilot 2nd Lt. Paul R. Gruhn and ball-turret gunner Staff Sgt. Dale T. Butt are buried in Wisconsin.

The loss of Howe's bomber now

Unteroffizier Bernhard Kunze of 1./JG 1 proudly standing next to the rudder of his FW 190 A-5 410055, on which five victory symbols have been applied. This fifth victory was B-17F 42-30068 of the 388th Bomb Group. ROB W. DE VISSER

raises the question about the availability of friendly fighter escort. How was it possible that Howe's B-17 was jumped by German fighters and was not assisted in any way by friendly ones? If friendly fighters had been available to Howe, there would have been no reason for him to go to lower altitude to escape from the German fighters. With the remaining three good engines, he could easily stayed out of the effective range of any light flak guns and especially those he now encountered near Haamstede. Most probably, he would have safely returned to Knettishall. What happened exactly?

The fighter escort for the wing was to be provided by the 4th and 78th Fighter Groups. The 4th Fighter Group put up forty-nine Thunderbolts; three of them had to return early. The group, led by Lt. Col. Donald J. M. Blakeslee, met the B-17s at mid-Channel. The B-17s were off course as we have seen. The P-47s took up positions slightly above the bombers and

The pilots of 8./JG 26 in Wevelghem, Belgium, in 1943. Fourth from right is
Feldwebel Erich Schwarz, one of the pursuers of Howe's B-17 over southern Holland
on August 19. ERIC MOMBEEK VIA DONALD L. CALDWELL

Deelen airfield, July 1943. *Unteroffizier* Bernhard Kunze and *Unteroffizier* Rudolf Hübl
of 1./JG 1 have received the Iron Cross, Second Class. Both claimed a B-17
destroyed near Haamstede on August 19. This was 42-30068 of the 388th Bomb
Group. ROB W. DE VISSER

remained with them until halfway between the primary and secondary target. Then course was set for Debden again "with no positive identification of enemy aircraft made," according to their report.

The 78th Fighter Group put up forty-eight Thunderbolts, of which four returned early. The group, led by Major Harry J. Dayhuff, also met the bombers at mid-Channel and remained above them until past Woensdrecht. However, pilots in this group did report some enemy aircraft over Tholen Island and engaged them immediately. One of the pilots was 1st Lt. Kenneth W. Dougherty of the 83rd Fighter Squadron:

> I was flying Trumpcard White 3, at an altitude of 26,000 feet over Woensdrecht. As we made a turn to port I saw four Me 109s below at eight o'clock flying in widely separated elements of two. They were at six o'clock on the B-17s. I called Capt Davis that there were bandits below, so he replied, "Let's go get 'em." I started after the last two. I was coming down out of the sun, the bandits at this time were at three o'clock low. I was well into my bounce when four Me 109s flew directly across me at about fifty yards ahead. I fired a two second burst at them as I pulled up to avoid a collision. I skidded up into a climbing turn and came back down on their tail. I was about 800 yards away and they were making a diving turn to port. I closed to about 500 yards and fired a two second burst and saw incendiary flashes on the starboard wing. I kept closing and firing, but observed no hits. The 109s then started a climbing turn to port and I closed rapidly to about 200 yards and fired a three second burst and observed incendiary flashes on both wings and on the fuselage, immediately aft of the cockpit. I then closed to about 100 yards and fired a five second burst. Smoke poured out of his starboard oil cooler. He mushed forward and then dropped like a stone out of my sight under my nose. I then broke sharply away, cleared my tail, and rolled over to look for him, but didn't see him, so I started for home.

The combat took place over Woensdrecht at 1900 hours.

The gun-camera film that Kenneth Dougherty brought back to Duxford and the supporting statement of his wing man brought him the award of the first of three air combat victories he was able to achieve. His flight leader, Capt. Jesse C. Davis, did fire a burst at one of the Me 109s, but missed. The German loss list, however, does not contain a likely candidate for Dougherty's victory.

The final resting place for four crewmembers of B-17F 42-30068 in the Long Island National Cemetery, Farmingdale, New York.

Within the 83rd Fighter Squadron, Red Flight had watched while White Flight went into action. First Lieutenant Don Bodenhamer, Jr., reported:

> I was leading Trumpcard Red Flight. When White Flight went in to bounce four Me 109s, I observed two Me 109s coming in behind them and at the same time and level, flying in the same direction as the enemy aircraft that White Flight was bouncing. I pulled over and went down on the last two ships. They saw me start my bounce, so they immediately went into a dive. With everything forward I had difficulty in catching one of them and was closing slowly. I began firing at about 650 yards and continued from line astern until I broke away at about 350 or 400 yards. I fired over 500 rounds in a series of several bursts and observed hits on the right wing.

His claim for an Me 109 damaged was awarded due to a supporting statement by his wing man.

At this stage of the mission, there was apparently plenty of friendly fighter cover available for unfortunate Lieutenant Howe. However, now the reports start to become vague and inconclusive in their remarks.

Colonel Russell Wilson, the staff officer of the 4th Bomb Wing who conducted the post-mission critique, remarked: "The fighter cover we had was up there but it didn't interfere with a reasonable number of enemy planes that attacked us." The after-action report of the wing put it even more bluntly: "The fighter rendezvous was made on time, but in the opinion of

our crews, the fighters flew too high
to be of assistance to our bombers
during the few attacks that developed." And: "One bomber which was
damaged by fighters was forced to fall
below the formation where it was
immediately attacked by six or eight
FW 190s. However, the P-47s in our
fighter cover made no effort to dive
down to assist the distressed aircraft."

Combat wing commander Colonel
Old, who had flown in the same
squadron as unfortunate Benjamin
Howe and his crew, reported: "Six
fighters came in to our left as we were
coming out and made one pass at us I
could see. The P-47s were circling
above and the only thing they accomplished was to get a grandstand seat
to watch the fight."

Staff Sgt. Stephen A. Toth, radio
operator, killed in action on his third
operational mission. THOMAS G. TOTH

To summarize: the bombers crews
were not very satisfied with their "lit-
tle friends" on this occasion and saw Howe being pounded by the FW 190s
after he dropped from the formation, without the P-47s coming to his rescue. This now poses the question of what these fighter groups reported
about this episode of their mission upon their return. In the Fighter Command narrative of operations, the following remark is made in the para-
graph dealing with the exploits of the 4th Fighter Group: "A red flare was
seen from a B-17 as the Group left them but they were not being attacked.
No positive identification of enemy aircraft was made." And in the para-
graph about the 78th Fighter Group: "One straggler, with one engine smoking, seen leaving formation."

Most probably, the B-17 firing the red flare was Howe's; there is no
doubt that he was the straggler that the 78th Fighter Group observed.
Apparently, in both instances, the German fighters that fell upon this prey
immediately after it left the formation were not spotted by the fighter pilots,
as they were by the bomber crews. It is likely that the limited fuel supply of
the Thunderbolts prevented both groups from sending a flight of P-47s with
Howe for his return trip "just in case." Whatever the reasons might have
been, Howe had to run the gauntlet alone, and he finally lost to the combined effect of German flak and fighters.

All other bomber crews safely returned to their respective home bases in England. Without having dropped their bombs, they had another mission chalked up towards the magical number of twenty-five and thus the ticket home. For them, this had been a true milk run. Not so for Howe's crew: eight men were killed, two sat bewildered in a German cell.

The next day, a post-mission critique took place in which the commanding officers of all bomb groups received a severe dressing-down from Col. Russell A. Wilson. Wilson was especially critical about the formations that had been flown, as the following excerpts from that meeting demonstrate:

> About the best formation all day was when a ship caught fire and dove down, and his two wingmen went with him. [This referred to *Black Heart Jr* of the 96th Bomb Group, which went down during assembly over England.]
>
> The 96th was strung out, even the leader's element. The leader of the second element dropped back a quarter of a mile. The 388th were to one side and strung well back. The squadron furnished by the 401st Combat Wing was strung back out of sight. No one was worse than any other—you were all bad. I thought it was a good idea to run new crews on these missions, but if they have this idea about spreading all over the sky because of friendly fighter support, we had better start them on a raid to Bremen or Berlin. Today was the poorest defensive formation I ever saw.
>
> The fact that we were flying composite groups is no excuse for the fact that the six plane squadrons did not stay together. Group and combat wing commanders must indoctrinate crews, including new crews to stay in defensive formation *at all times* on a combat mission.

In his report about the mission to the Eighth Air Force headquarters, which was submitted four days after the meeting, he put it all somewhat more mildly: "The formation flown by the lead group on this mission was not satisfactory, especially on the route back. The aircraft were too spread out to be considered as proper defensive. This might have been disastrous had many enemy aircraft been encountered."

He also made the following remarks:

> 1. There are two explanations for the unsatisfactory formation flown on this mission. Each group was, of necessity, a composite of aircraft of three or more bombardment groups of this command, and as such demonstrated the inherent disadvantages of composite groups

for formation flying. In addition, the majority of crews were made up of unseasoned replacements, many of whom were participating in their first mission.

2. To help improve our defensive tactics, combat wing and group commanders have been directed to intensify the training of new crews in formation flying.

3. Again it is gratifying to note the lack of abortives resulting from engineering, armament or equipment failures. This splendid accomplishment reflects the highest credit on the combat and ground crews of all groups of this command.

CHAPTER 8

Aftermath

THE PRISONERS OF WAR

Twenty-two shot-down American airmen spent the night of August 19 in a prison cell in Holland. Only a few hours ago, these men were safe and sound on their bases in England. Stunned and sometimes wet and in shock, they had to come to terms with the fact that they were now prisoners of war. These are the experiences of 1st Lt. Dwight M. Curo, the navigator of Lieutenant Nix's B-17 of the 303rd Bomb Group. His account, which starts just after he was captured, may represent that of the other captives:

It was by now nearly dark, and at a word from our guards we started back toward the small town [Raamsdonksveer]. Buck and myself leading the procession along the narrow little road, well covered by the six weapons of our captors. After about half an hour, we reached the little hamlet and were taken to the local jail. As we approached I noticed soldiers removing parachutes and flying equipment from a truck before the door, and as we entered the building I caught a glimpse of a couple of our crew under guard in an adjoining building. It looked as though they had had no better luck than ourselves in getting away. But, really, under the circumstances, escape had been impossible. The nature of the country coupled by the fact that we had been very visible in our parachutes for quite some time precluded any such thing as evasion. I learned later from some of the boys that the Germans had been waiting for them as they hit the ground.

And thus began a very trying period for us all. The next ten days were to be nightmares of hunger and discomfort. We were held in the jail office for about two hours. During that time, we were not allowed to smoke or to have water. Sergeant Gross's burned face gave him considerable pain and Sergeant Buck was in a state of collapse. Most of the boys looked pretty forlorn. At length one of the Dutch civil police officers acceded to my repeated requests and got

181

us a little water, although the German soldiers present did not seem
to like the idea. Eventually, there was a commotion in the hallway
outside and we heard a motor outside.

A German officer came in with a couple of satelite non-coms. He
was evidently quite somebody, because all the Nazis "popped to" and
the Sergeant who was in charge of our guard came through with a
very snappy salute and a big "Heil Hitler." I can remember being
very amused and damn near laughed in spite of my low spirits. It was
an exact duplicate of any movie scene. Incidentally, that is the first
and last time that I have seen such upraised arm or fol-de-rol about
Hitler; the *Luftwaffe* with whom we have been mostly in contact seem
to content themselves with the regular military salute. This officer
evidently came to make disposition of us, for we were taken outside
and put into a truck; our guards lined themselves around the open
outer rails and sat with drawn pistols watching us closely. It must
have been about 2300 hours or half an hour later when we completed our truck ride through several small towns, along tree lined
paved roads and turned off at last through a guarded gate and
stopped before a camouflaged low brick building in a sparse growth
of trees. From the little that was observable, this was evidently part of
a military garrison or air field. We were herded inside and thus saw
our first German prison. The interior was dim and poorly lighted.
Bars and barred gates seemed to block our passage but at length one
of these was opened and we were led single file down the narrow
dim passage way. It was a gruesome place. The guards seemed to be
dirty, ill-uniformed and ignorant, though they did not threaten or
mistreat us. The doors lining either side appeared to be very thick
and sturdy with metal hasps securing them and small peepholes
about an inch in diameter bored through them at eye-level. It was all
in all, a real dungeon and my heart sank at the thought of incarcera-
tion, but tried to put on a brave face for the benefit of my comrades
and to deny any possible satisfaction to our captors. Up to this
time, we had not been allowed to talk, but we had been together.
Lieutenant Moffatt, his head bandaged, a severe laceration in his
scalp, Sergeants Gross, Perez, Boyd had all joined up at the little
Dutch jail where we were first taken. They, like Sergeant Buck and
myself, had been captured immediately.

We were now put into individual cells. The heavy door shut
behind me and the lock rattled as our guard fastened it. The interior of the cell was of heavy brick; a sturdy wooden bench its only
furnishing. No mattress, no blankets, no nothing. The lights were

"Missing in Action." Fifty-two of these telegrams were sent after Mission 85, including one to the family of Tech Sgt. Russell G. Chester, radio operator of B-17F 42-3101.
RUSSELL G. CHESTER

then switched off from outside and I was left in complete blackness. From high up in the corner a little light was visible through an aperture about six inches square. This seemed to be the only window. By this time, my nerves were beginning to untwine themselves somewhat, and I dazedly grouped my way to the bench and sat down. It was quite cold and my only clothing was a thin flying suit over my olive-drab uniform. My thoughts at this time were pretty black. I lay on the bench and tried to sleep, but it was impossible. My mind was in a whirl of dispair. Little noises in the darkness identified themselves as mice or rats. I lay and shivered. From a nearby cell came the sound of whimpering and crying. I think it was Sergeant Buck, but am not sure. Sure as hell didn't blame him much—felt just like that myself; but I did call out to him to buck up and he ceased.

That was one hell of a night. From time to time, the lights would be switched on from outside and the guards would peek through the little hole in the door, presumably to see that we had not disappeared. Where or how we would have gotten out of that dungeon I don't know, I felt like a rat in a trap or an animal on exhibition.

Leonard Spivey of the 381st Bomb Group, who had landed in the middle of Schiedam, recalled what was prominent in his mind that first night:

> There is no question that the worst thing I had to contend with dur-
> ing all the time flying combat or as a prisoner of war was the
> thought of the War Department telegram to my mother. I'm sure
> the feeling had to be the same with all shot down flyers. It hit me

> when I was alone for the first time
> after being captured. Standing
> there in that tiny cell, I imagined
> the anguish that would come to
> my mother and father. How I
> wished there was some way they
> could know that I was alright and
> that I was determined to survive
> and get back home. Some days
> later, I was given the opportunity
> to send a *Kriegsgefangenen* post-
> card. Seeing my brief note of
> assurance in my own handwriting
> hopefully would raise their spirits.
>   Upon returning home, I
> learned that the whole family had
> been considerably shaken, my
> brothers and sisters too, and all in
> a pretty bad state from the time of
> the missing in action-notice until
> they knew I was alive and a pris-
> oner of war, which was a period of
> about six weeks. My father was

Dwight M. Curo as a POW. A drawing
by fellow prisoner Ernest E. Warsaw
for his wartime log. MARY M. MCINTYRE

> devastated and believed the worst; my mother never gave up hope.
> It took a couple of months for my post card to get to them. This was
> not an unusual interval for family and loved ones to be kept in a
> state of terrible waiting. In many cases it was much worse.

Upon hearing the news that his brother Orlando was missing, Robert
Koenig tried to raise the spirits of his parents and immediately wrote from
the U.S. Naval Training Station in Farragut, Idaho:

> But, for some reason or other, I just can't believe that Orlo is gone.
> I have the faithful believe that he is safe and alive somewhere, prob-

A new load of American prisoners is herded into a German tram. The picture was obviously taken after the men were interrogated in Dulag Luft, as the sign on the tram window indicates that it ran from Frankfurt to Oberursel, where Dulag Luft was located. BUNDESARCHIV

ably a prisoner, and I'll keep on thinking that until I hear otherwise. The chance of survival are quite good in a plane the size of his, and a good many of them, when forced down, make landings in enemy territory and are taken prisoner. That's what I think happened to Orlo and I hope that that is what you think. I just can't believe that my brother, who always seemed so sure of himself and able to take himself so well, would have anything else happen to him.

I do hope that you don't take this too hardly. I know that you realize that when people are defending something as big and as great as our country and way of life is, things like that are bound to happen, and you can be sure that what Orlo has done has been far more important than anything else he could have done if times were different. He wasn't just living the kind of a life we would all enjoy living, he was risking his own life so that other people may enjoy the advantages for which we're fighting.

Fortunately, Roberts's feeling were right; Orlando Koenig had indeed survived the demise of his bomber and was made prisoner of war.

The new surroundings: behind barbed wire and watch towers. DEBBIE MILLER HUGHES

Dwight Curo resumes his account in the early morning hours of August 20:

Morning came at last and some of the boys who requested it were given a cup of water and a piece of German bread. I, for my part, was not hungry so did not ask for anything to eat. As daylight entered the little grated "airhole" up in the corner of the cell I was able to discover writing and pictures drawn on the painted door and on the bench on which I sat. There were many of them, mostly French; evidently, my "apartment" was a popular place. In several spots, the inmates had marked off the length of their stay by a dash for each day. Some of the records were for as much as thirty days which gave me a real cause to worry. I felt that a man would go mad if cooped up in such a hole for so long. It must have been the state of my nerves which made me feel that way. I have learned since from experience and from the stories of others, that a man can stand conditions like that for longer than he thinks if he can control himself. Nonetheless, solitary confinement is a horrible experience. The worst punishment that I know. Fortunately, as it turned out, our stay was to end that day.

Most of the men were first transported to Amsterdam by rail and then
all of them went to Frankfurt. The
Germans called their interrogation
center near this city Durchgangslager
der Luftwaffe; it became known to the
Americans as Dulag Luft.

After interrogation in Dulag Luft
the new prisoners were sent to various
camps, called Stammlager, or Stalag
for short. The officers and enlisted
men were separated now. The officers
were sent to Stalag Luft III near
Sagan, a camp especially for air force
officers in present day Poland. Most
enlisted men ended up in Stalag
XVIIB near Krems in Austria, after
a two months's stay in Stalag VIIA
in Moosburg, north of Munich in
Germany.

Second Lt. Joel H. Tutt and his wife,
Ruth, in Las Vegas, Nevada, in 1943.
JOEL H. TUTT

Now the long, long wait for the
liberation began. Through the Y.M.C.A. and the Red Cross, most of the prisoners received "a wartime log" to be used for stories, poems, drawings, and
more. I was lucky during my research to be able to read and view several of
these of the men who were shot down on August 19, 1943.

It is fitting to capture the events of the twenty long months from early September 1943 to May 1945 by quoting several entries from the wartime log of
Joel Tutt, the bombardier of Lieutenant Howe's B-17 of the 388th Bomb
Group. Tutt wrote it as a sort of diary, telling the story to his wife Ruth, who was
waiting for him in Monticello, Georgia. It will become clear that food, mail, the
weather, and boredom were key words for the prisoners for those many
months to come. Tutt's first entry is about how he got hold of his confidant.

December 11, 1943
With the aid of a can of jam and one-and-a-half bars of chocolate, I
managed to trade a fellow out of this war log through whose pages
I hope to give you an idea of camp life.

December 21, 1943
My happiest day since I've been down. I received two letters—one
written in Monticello, Georgia, October 5, and the other one from

St. Petersburg, Florida, October 17. You were speaking of chicken pie and lambchops. I'm glad that you can have the good meals and that you need two blankets and could have many more. We have three and could use ten, but knowing that it is me and not you makes the three blankets do the work.

December 30, 1943
Today Pilley and I have been busy getting crackers ground, potatoes washed and various jobs done as tomorrow we start our week of cooking. The Germans gave us some beer for New Year. I saw a show tonight that was as good as any I've ever seen. It was on the order of "Hell's-a-poppin." The boys at the theater surely work hard to give us entertainment.

January 15, 1944
Just finished a few rubbers of bridge. Been raining all day so we have been inside. There are some old copies of *McCall's* magazine here and we have been looking them over. They help us to remember how people live on the outside of the fence. Life gets pretty monotonous inside the fence, especially in this kind of weather.

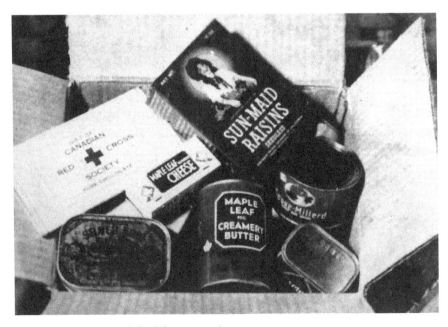

A Red Cross parcel. DEBBIE MILLER HUGHES

January 23, 1944 (written by Arthur Pilley)
Tutt has had it. He has a touch of the flu that is sweeping the barracks; four in hospital and about eight in bed. Joe is staying in bed fighting it off. Getting a bit colder out.

February 3, 1944
Well, Pilley and I finished our week of cooking tonight. I can truly sympathize with a housewife with a large family. Received a letter from you this morning. Also wrote to Irvin for membership of the Caterpillar Club and to send you the pin.

February 15, 1944
This day has found me rather busy. I took a shower this morning, shaved, made me a clipboard out of some Red Cross boxes and asorted the potatoes. I put another verse or two in the log tonight. We have the phonograph in our barracks tonight. There are some good records like "There will never be another you" which is playing now. Each record brings back a memory. The mailman missed me again today. Air raid tonight. Imagine it was Berlin.

March 12, 1944
Another week has gone by. This is one place I like to see the time go in a hurry. We woke up this morning to find it snowing. It did not last very long, I'm glad to say. It was very disagreeable at appel.

April 18, 1944
A rainy afternoon in Germany, it has been a dark gloomy day which is very disagreeable. We have been very lucky for the past few days because we really had some good weather. I have been in for most of the day except for some time which Hasson and I walked around the perimeter. Sure enjoy having Hasson to talk to because we have something in common. Dick Loveless received thirteen letters today. Forney received his first mail. The mailman missed me again today. My thoughts as usual have been of you and home. How glad I'll be when we get out of this barbed wire hell. It could be much worse but it gets mighty tiresome the same thing day after day. No one can ever know what it is like until one experiences it. If it were not for the many pleasant memories made possible by you this place would really be hell. We had another air raid this afternoon.

April 28, 1944
I certainly had a nice day in the way of mail. I received thirteen letters and a picture. The picture is my prize possession now. I've been

wishing for some ever since I've been here. The letters were as follows: one from mother, one from D., one from Martha Smith, and ten from you. It has been cloudy and cold today, very miserable. A fire would really feel good.

May 8, 1944
This has been a November day instead of a May day. It has been dark, damp, dreary and cold all day and still is. We could really use a fire today but we are on summer ration of coal and it does not permit us to use our valuable coal supply. It was so cold in our classroom we could hardly write. I am still trying the math but it gets harder every day. We received clean bed linen today, the first in weeks.

June 6, 1944
We heard at 1:30 PM today of the invasion. So far the news has been slow and not much in detail. I hope and pray that it is a success and we do not lose too many men. Maybe it won't be long before this war is over. Chuck Forney, a combine mate, starts cooking for Schaefer, another combine mate, for the duration. The wager was: Schaefer was to cook until the invasion, Forney was to cook from the invasion to the end of the war. The funny part was that the wager was made only two and a half days ago.

July 13, 1944
We are really crowded now. Our block is up to 136 men. It was crowded with 102 men, so we thought. I imagine before long we will be even more crowded. The worst part about it is the cooking arrangements. You can imagine trying to cook for sixty-eight men on a stove about the size of a water heater.

August 5, 1944
What a surprise I had today. I received two letters from you and one from mother, but the best of all was the pictures. You can never know how much they mean to me. It was a good thing they came because I was just about to go nuts. Soon I will have been down a year and have only received the one picture of you and one of the folks. But now life is 500 percent better. I worked all day making frames for the pictures.

August 20, 1944
We fixed a super meal yesterday for two occasions: first, our anniversary, and second, it was the first year as "Kriegies" for Miller, Pilley,

and me. A year ago last night I could have certainly used that meal as I was weary, hungry, aching and sore. A lot has happened since then. A few days in the "jug" at Amsterdam and Frankfurt and then my entry into Center Camp Stalag Luft III, Sagan. I have seen the seasons, removal of the British from this camp and the growth from a few hundred to 1,500. The place has taught me tolerance, appreciation of the little things of life and countless other things. In closing, I am hoping and praying that this war will soon cease and the world can once more know the word Peace.

Unfortunately for Tutt and the others, there were still a long autumn and winter ahead of them. A dramatic turn in the dull events came on Saturday night, January 27, 1945, when all prisoners at Stalag Luft III were ordered to be ready to march in just two hours. With the Russian armies rapidly advancing from the east, the Germans had decided to move the prisoners south, to Stalag VIIA, near Moosburg. This was the camp where most of the enlisted men shot down on August 19, 1943, had been held the first two months. Tutt did not write in his diary in this period, but recorded the events on little scraps of paper:

Ralph Miller made this drawing in his wartime log. It shows his impression of the last moments of *Lady Liberty* over Flushing. ROGER V. MILLER

On the night of January 27 at 9:00 PM, we were told that we would evacuate in two hours. By 11:45, we had our stuff ready to move in the form of blanket rolls, crude knapsacks and some even had sleds. Everyone was plenty excited and full of uncertain anticipation.

After being counted and much waiting we pulled out at 4:45 AM on January 28 on foot. On leaving, our senior allied officer gave us a word of cheer. We were given all the Red Cross food we could carry.

We made 17 km to a town Halbau, our first day. At Halbau we slept in a beautiful church. I must say we were crowded though, 1,700 men in a building. The march that day was in bad weather, snow storms and temperature about 13 degrees below zero.

January 29, 1945
Left Halbau at 9:00 AM, marched to Freiwaldau and 8 km where we stayed in an old barn about the size of our warehouse. However, only 480 slept in this barn, the others moved on to another barn down the road. The roads were cluttered with evacuees. War is sure an awful thing.

January 30, 1945
Still at the same barn. The rest is helping us a lot, but we are cold as we have only one blanket. Everyone is making it fine. Took inventory on our food and have about a two weeks supply of close rations. East Camp passed today.

January 31, 1945
Got up at 5:00 AM, heard we were to do 30 km today. Left the barn at 7:00 AM. We made a sled to carry our food on.

February 1, 1945
We were a tired bunch of fellows when we arrived at Muskau. Slept in a pottery factory. The best place we have stayed in yet. We even have heat. It is a good thing as we were soaking wet last night. We are all in good spirits after a good night's rest and some food. Received ¼ loaf bread per man from Germans, the first since leaving camp. It is 10:00 AM and looks like we will be here for another day. Hope so, anyway.

So far our guards have treated us well and the civilians have even given us drinks along the road. If we can do as well in the future as

we have been in the past, we will make it okay, otherwise I'm afraid
to say what the outcome will be.

February 2, 1945
We are expecting some barley now. Have been ready to move again.
Met a fellow from Gainesville this morning. Traded Nescafe for
bread. The day turned out to be rather nice. Snow melting. Won't
be able to use sleds tomorrow.

February 3, 1945
Got up at 4:15 AM. Departed 8:20. Seems as if it is going to be a
warm day. Arrived at Graustein 3:00 PM. Sleeping in another barn. It
is muddy and sloppy as hell but looks like we will have plenty of
room.

February 4, 1945
Left about 7:30 AM for Spremberg. Arrived 10:30 (8 km). Stopped at
an army post. We are waiting to catch the train. 11:45 supposed to
get food. Received some soup. Boarded box car at 4:30 PM.

February 8, 1945
Since the 4th, it has been a nightmare.

February 12, 1945
At last we are at our destination I hope. We will exist.

The week-long train journey had now taken them to the south of Germany. Life was miserable in Moosburg. The camp was very crowded, with sometimes hundreds of men to a tent or barrack. The first concern was food. Tutt wrote on March 3: "We talk, think and dream of food."

Luckily, the ordeal was nearly over. On April 29, elements of the 14th Armored Division of General Patton's Third Army liberated the camp after a brief skirmish. After another week in Moosburg, Tutt and the others were deloused, then taken by a truck to the nearby airfield at Straubing. From here, they were taken by C-47s to Camp Lucky Strike near Le Havre in France. Tutt landed here on May 9. Five days later, he boarded the USS *Lejeune* and arrived safely in the United States. The twenty-one others that were captured on August 19, 1943, also survived their captivity and were reunited with their families in the United States.

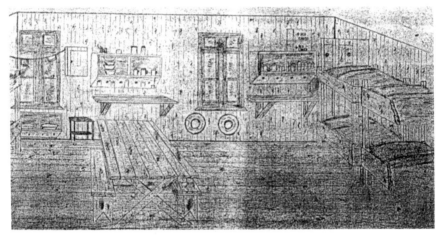

Barracks in Stalag Luft III and part of its interior, drawn by Ralph R. Miller in his wartime log.

THE TARGETS

As already mentioned in the previous chapters, the overall result of the August 19, 1943, mission had been very disappointing for the Americans. No bombs had been dropped on the primary targets in Brussels and Woens-drecht, due to cloud cover. The bombs that were dropped on the target of opportunity in Flushing and on the primary target in Gilze-Rijen had mostly missed and had killed many Dutch civilians. Also on the debit side were the five B-17s and one P-47 with their crews listed as missing in action and the B-17 that had crashed in England.

The Dutch government in exile had a special liaison officer for the Allied Air Forces at its staff at the embassy in London. He was naval Capt. Cornelis Moolenburgh. In his report to the Dutch minister of warfare, dated August 27, he stated:

Stalag VIIA near Moosburg, just after its liberation.
DEBBIE MILLER HUGHES

The daylight attacks in this period were confined to two attacks each on the airfields near Flushing and Woensdrecht, one attack on the airfield near Gilze-Rijen and one attack on the aircraft-factory "De Schelde" in Flushing. Both attacks on the Flushing airfield were executed by Fortresses of 8th Bomber Command, just like the attack on Gilze-Rijen.

It would go too far to describe these attacks in detail in this report. Suffice to say that all attacks were one great fiasco and as far as observed most of the bombs landed one to three miles from the airfields.

I talked about these attacks with Lieutenant Colonel Douglas. He did not express himself about this topic. He carefully took down what I told him and what I showed him, based on a map with the annotated bomb hits. He promised to brief General Eaker about it, after which he would inform me.

I emphasized to this American officer that it is not so much the damage that has been done, which prompted me to try to get information about the events. The most important thing is that the Dutch population loses their faith in the ability of the Allied air forces, when they learn about attacks on airfields with large formations of bombers, but at the same time observe how their bombs hit miles from these targets. This now causes the enemy to broadcast that the Anglo-Americans bombed villages in southwestern Holland "at random," as a result of which twenty-six Dutch civilians died.

Especially since the weather conditions were good, at Flushing only slight flak was encountered and near Gilze-Rijen German aircraft were encountered, whose attacks were classified as "mediocre," better results could have been expected. This is, unless the Fortress crews experienced the German resistance for the first time and that the Dutch targets were thus used as a "nursery slope," which is against all written orders by General Eaker.

British Air-Commodore Pendred also didn't have a reasonable explanation for the failure of the American bombing. He was also very much surprised about the choice of the Flushing airfield as a target. At this time this is of no value compared to other airfields, more inland, so that he inclined to the view that a practice target had been selected.

What the exact impact of his report to General Eaker's staff was is difficult to say. The facts, however, show that Flushing was not attacked again by the Eighth Air Force for the remainder of the war.

Ex-prisoners are ready to board C-47s of the 442nd Troop Carrier Group and depart for Camp Lucky Strike near Le Havre, France. LOUIS T. MOFFATT

Gilze-Rijen is quite a different story. Because of its importance for the German *Luftwaffe*, it remained on the American target list. Two months after the mission covered in this book, on October 20, sixteen B-17s of the 379th Bomb Group attacked the airfield as a "target of opportunity." Cloud cover had prevented them from bombing their primary target at Düren in Germany. Again, the bombs fell outside the airfield boundary. Then the Americans reverted to another tactic. On December 4, sixteen P-47s of the 353rd Fighter Group executed a dive-bombing attack on the airfield. Slight damage was the result.

On December 23, January 23, January 25, and January 31, similar attacks took place, all with minor damage as a result. Thus it became apparant that this too was not the best way to put an airfield out of action. The heavies were called in again. On February 10, 1944, eighty-one B-24s of various bomb groups of the Second Bomb Division were scheduled to attack the airfield. Over England very poor weather conditions caused several aircraft crashes, twenty-six American airmen losing their lives. The weather over Gilze-Rijen was very poor as well. Snow showers and cloud prevented accurate bombing and only twenty-seven B-24s released their load. Two of the three runways were well hit. Some damage was also done to the village of Gilze. Luckily, only one civilian was killed. On February 14, forty-six P-47s executed another dive-bombing attack, when they found their primary target at Eindhoven obscured by clouds. As a result, the Germans had to suspend operations for about four days.

Then the medium bombers tried their luck. The bomb groups equipped with the Marauder had been transferred from the Eighth to the Ninth Air Force. On February 22, sixty Marauders of the 386th Bomb Group from Great Dunmow were dispatched to bomb Gilze-Rijen. Much damage was done, but two Marauders were shot down by flak from Gilze-Rijen. Two days later, the Marauders repeated their successful performance, this time forty bombers dropped their bombs on the airfield.

On March 19, twenty P-47s of the 78th Fighter Group came in for another dive-bombing attack, at least one runway was hit. And on May 2, it was thirty P-51 Mustang fighters who executed yet another such attack.

On May 31, twenty-three B-17s of the 303rd and 379th Bomb Groups dropped sixty-nine tons of bombs on the airfield. When they found their primary target at Colmar in France obscured by clouds, they made a large turn in northerly direction and selected Gilze-Rijen as a target of opportunity. All bombs fell within the airfield boundaries, but the exact extent of the damage is unknown.

Unfortunately, on July 5, the same groups encountered heavy cloud cover over Gilze-Rijen, which was assigned to them as primary target for that

day. Much had changed since August 19, 1943, and the American bombardiers were now able to "see through" the clouds by using GEE-H radar.
So despite the clouds, the thirty-eight bombers dropped their 105 tons of
bombs. Although many bombs indeed hit the airfield, more than 200 bombs
struck the village of Gilze. Much damage was done, and unfortunately,
twenty-one civilians were killed.

The last American bombs fell on the airfield on August 7, when an
unknown B-24 unit dropped them after turning away from its primary target
in northern France. All bombs fell in the fields to the south of the airfield,
killing four civilians.

The end for Gilze-Rijen as an active German base came on August 15
and September 3. On both days, the Royal Air Force executed daylight missions to the airfield with Lancaster and Halifax bombers. This time the Germans were unable to properly repair the damage. This, combined with the
swift advance of the Allied armies through Belgium, caused the Germans to
evacuate the field. The very next day they demolished everything that wasn't
already destroyed by the bombs and left the base, to the immense relief of
the Dutch population. Eventually, the villages were liberated on October 27,
after some brief skirmishes.

THE EIGHTH AIR FORCE

At the end of this book, we will very briefly look at the Eighth Air Force
after Mission 85. The crews that had returned were given a few days' rest.
On the twenty-fourth, they went on the warpath again, this time to airfields
near Paris. This proved to be the milk run that Mission 85 on August 19
had promised to be before take-off. Only one B-17 was lost, but all but one
of its crew were picked up by Allied Air-Sea Rescue. The first major attack
on a target in Germany itself again was on September 6. The mission, to
Stuttgart, turned into a fiasco. Again the weather interfered in keeping
proper formations and in the bombing itself. No fewer than forty-five B-17s
were lost, although twelve of these ditched in the North Sea and all twelve
crews were picked up by Air-Sea Rescue. After the costly missions to Schweinfurt and Regensburg the overall strength of the Eighth Air Force was seriously depleted. For the remainder of that month the Eighth Air Force
gathered strength and in October several major missions were flown. On
three days running, October 8, 9, and 10, large-scale attacks were executed
on Bremen, Anklam/Marienburg/Gdynia, and Münster, respectively. Again
losses were severe, but the bombing results in itself seemed to be encouraging. After a brief rest, Schweinfurt, that dreaded target, was on the mission
list again, on October 14. As feared, the German reaction was fierce and
sixty B-17s were lost.

Only ten minutes after returning from the harrowing mission to Oschersleben on January 11, 1944, mission leaders Lt. Col. William Calhoun, in the center, and Brig. Gen. Robert F. Travis shake hands under the lead ship, B-17F 41-24635 *The 8 Ball Mk II.* On the right is assistant lead navigator Darrell D. Gust, who finished his tour of operations that day. DARRELL D. GUST

Another important development that month was the operational debut of the twin-engined P-38 Lightning for escort duties. With its range, it could protect the bombers longer from enemy fighters than the P-47 and thus help diminish the losses. However, their engines frequently gave them trouble in the poor European weather and the fighter never became a huge success.

November saw several epic missions, all worth a book in themselves. On November 3, Wilhelmshaven was bombed; on the fifth, Gelsenkirchen; on the eleventh, Münster; on the thirteenth, twenty-sixth, and twenty-ninth, Bremen. Most of these missions were executed in very poor and extremely cold weather conditions.

On December 11, when the bombers attacked Emden, the P-51 Mustang fighter operated for the first time as escort fighter. Looking back, it may be said that this was the definite turning point in the war between the Eighth Air Force and the *Luftwaffe*. The fighters were now able to escort the bombers to any target and back, the concept of the bomber defending itself was now left. Later, when the *Luftwaffe* was hesitant to come up and fight, the American fighters went down to the "deck," in order to search for airfields and the *Luftwaffe* and "strafe" them. This finally broke the back of the *Luftwaffe*. However, its pilots remained dangerous and deadly opponents in the months to come, when the Mustang was not available in large numbers. On January 11, 1944, the target was Oschersleben. The heaviest German opposition since Schweinfurt was met and exactly the same number of bombers was lost—sixty. The 303rd Bomb Group lost eleven of its B-17s. The lead pilot for the group was Lt. Col. William Calhoun in his faithful *The 8 Ball Mk II.* Calhoun had returned to England to serve as executive officer on the staff of the 41st Combat Wing and to fly more combat missions. That same day, Col. James Howard, a Mustang pilot, gained a Congressional Medal of Honor for his effort in single-handedly breaking up a major German attack on a combat wing. He was the only fighter pilot in the European theater to receive America's highest award for valor.

In February, the Eighth Air Force gave high priority to attacks on the aircraft industry, this with the oncoming invasion of Western Europe in mind. During "Big Week," from February 20 to 25, several major aircraft factories were bombed. Both Schweinfurt and Regensburg were among the targets. Again, the Eighth Air Force suffered heavy losses, but the factories bombed were well hit, and the *Luftwaffe* that came up to defend them also suffered heavily.

A psychological turning point was reached on March 6, when the first large-scale attack on the German capital Berlin was made. Despite the loss of sixty-nine bombers, its highest single day loss of the war, the Eighth Air Force returned to Berlin again on March 8 and 9, thus showing that it had not just been a one-day "show" for publicity.

In May, with the *Luftwaffe* now severely depleted, the "oil offensive" started. After the war, this was considered to be the most effective choice of a target system. For the bomber crews, the oil refineries were a very rewarding target, as the huge columns of smoke gave firsthand evidence of good bombing. However, the Germans protected their precious refineries with a large number of flak batteries, and for example, Merseburg became as well-known and dreaded as Schweinfurt.

Also in May, June, and July, many missions to France were flown, either in preparation or support of the invasion on June 6 or to bomb the V-weapon sites.

In France, Harry T. Lay was killed. Lay, who had been the *ad hoc* lead pilot of the combat wing attacking Gilze-Rijen on August 19, 1943, had safely finished his tour of operations. He then transferred to the 78th Fighter Group flying P-47s "to shoot back at the Jerries for a change." On July 18, 1944, while strafing a troop train in France, his P-47 was hit by flak. Lay bailed out, but was killed by German troops from the train he had just attacked. He is buried in the American Military Cemetery in Epinal, France.

In September, the Eighth Air Force flew many missions over Holland, in support of Operation Market Garden, the ambitious plan to capture several bridges over Dutch waterways and open the road for the ground troops into Germany. On September 17, large-scale bombing of flak positions along the route for the gliders and paratroop-carrying aircraft took place. Later, the B-24s executed highly dangerous low-level resupply missions for the fighting paratroopers on the ground. Many fighter groups flew lethal 'flak-suppression missions. The 56th Fighter Group, for example, lost six-teen P-47s on September 18, although seven of the pilots were able to crash their ships behind friendly lines.

On the first day of Market Garden, Maj. Klaus Mietusch, the *Grup-penkommandeur* of III./JG 26, was killed. His death typified the enormous pressure that was exercised on the *Luftwaffe*. For its pilots, there were no lim-its to their tours of operations and they were confronted with an ever increasing number of Allied planes. Mietusch had flown 452 combat mis-sions, in which he had shot down seventy-two aircraft, including the B-17 of Lieutenant Nix and his crew of the 303rd Bomb Group on August 19, 1943. Now this experienced ace fell to the guns of a Mustang of the 361st Fighter Group, one of the no fewer than fifteen operational fighter groups that the Eighth Air Force now had available.

That the *Luftwaffe* remained a lethal opponent at times and chose a place to attack where this Allied fighter escort was not available was demon-strated on September 27. The B-24s of the Second Bomb Division were heading for Kassel, when the 445th Bomb Group temporarily strayed out of the bomber stream and its protective fighter escort. They were struck by an overwhelming force of German fighters and in just minutes twenty-five Lib-erators were shot down. The very next day, the 303rd Bomb Group was hit by a similar mass of German fighters and before its own fighter escort could intervene eleven of its B-17s were lost.

In December, the Germans executed their last desperate attempt to reconquer the ground that was lost by attacking through the Ardennes. The Battle of the Bulge at the end of that month brought the Eighth Air Force out in strength. On December 24, their largest effort of the war was launched: no less than 2,046 heavy bombers attacked airfields, marshalling yards, and communication centers in western Germany.

In 1945, German resistance collapsed and the Allied air forces overflew the country from end to end. The *Luftwaffe* was now nearly defeated, only the flak remained a feared opponent for the bomber crews.

The last combat mission, to targets in Czechoslovakia and in southeast-ern Germany, was flown on April 25. Six B-17s were lost to flak.

The last missions of the Eighth Air Force before hostilities officially ceased were flown to western Holland. With Holland split in half by the advancing Allied armies, the western part was deprived of food coming in from the eastern provinces. Thousands of civilians died from starvation and

"Many thanks."

it was decided that mercy missions were to be flown by the Royal Air Force and the Eighth Air Force. The Germans agreed not to fire on the low-flying Lancasters and B-17s, and for the Americans, Operation Chowhound commenced on May 1 and ended on May 7. One B-17 of the 95th Bomb Group was lost in the North Sea on that very last day, the cause of its engine fire is not certain. Unfortunately, only two of its crewmembers were rescued.

The general feelings of the Dutch population for the men of the Eighth Air Force are probably best summed up by that what was found by the bomber crews along one of the routes for the B-17s during Chowhound. Dutch civilians used thousands of cut-off flower heads to lay out two large words in some bulb fields. They simply said, "MANY THANKS."

Epilogue

In the postwar years, life resumed its normal course. The people in the Dutch villages that were hit rebuilt their homes and farms. The villages of East-Souburg and West-Souburg have now all but virtually been swallowed by ever-growing Flushing and Middelburg. There is no airfield there anymore and nothing reminds of the fateful days in August 1943. The same story goes for Hulten. A visitor to the village will find no evidence of the havoc that was created there in the early evening of August 19. Cafe Stad Parijs is restored and still in business along the Tilburg-Breda road, the farms are rebuilt and the vicinity is as peaceful as can be. Only in the tiny cemetery do several graves bear witness to the tragedies that befell some families so many years ago. Gilze-Rijen remains a busy military airfield. The Royal Netherlands Air Force has used the field since 1945 and will transform from an F-16 fighter base to the home base for squadrons equipped with Apache helicopters.

The Americans that survived the deadly air war also returned to normal life. Some made their career in the postwar United States Air Force, many returned to civilian life. Family life and careers kept most from thinking too much about the events of World War II. It was only in 1975 that the Eighth Air Force Historical Society was founded; it now has over 20,000 members. Together with this renewed interest in their past, many veterans returned to their former bases in England, where they spent such an impressive part of their lives. Some even made the trip to the continent to see the place where their plane had crashed and where they turned from warrior to prisoner of war. One of them was Joel Tutt, the bombardier and one of only two survivors of Lieutenant Howe's crew of the 388th Bomb Group. In 1981, he contacted a Dutch amateur air war historian, who arranged a trip to Haamstede for him and his wife, Ruth. Accompanied, among others, by two brothers of the Thuring family, who themselves had witnessed the crash of Lieutenant Nix's B-17 in Raamsdonksveer that same day, he visited the orchard where he landed with his parachute. Here he was met by several Dutch eyewitnesses of the crash of the bomber and his descent by parachute. One of these eyewitnesses sent his grandson to his house in order to get something. When the boy returned, he brought French franc banknotes with him. Tutt had handed them, part of his escape kit, to the man on August 19 in order to prevent them from falling into German hands. Now, thirty-four years later, he received most of them back. Then the meadow where the B-17 crashed and where eight of Joel's crew died was visited and homage was paid to their sacrifice.

Not only American veterans returned to meaningful places for them. *Luftwaffe* pilot Werner Möszner, who miraculously survived the unsuccessful belly-landing of his Me 109 near Waalwijk on August 19, also expressed the wish to visit the place where he nearly lost his life. In the summer of 1996, he and his wife visited this site, which has much changed since 1943, with me. Later that day, Möszner was flown over the site in a vintage Piper Cub, a remarkable experience for him after fifty-three years.

Not only veterans became interested in the past. Eldon F. Richter was the engineer of *Stric Nine* of the 303rd Bomb Group and was either killed during the German fighter attacks or drowned in the North Sea after bailing out of the stricken bomber. His body washed ashore on the Dutch coast on August 31 and was subsequently buried in the Heemskerk General Cemetery. After the war, his body was finally returned to his family in Waverly, Kansas. Eldon's brother Joe developed a great interest in the final months of

July 1996. Werner Möszner (second from right) and his wife on the site of his near fatal crash-landing in Waalwijk. Note the church, just visible between the buildings and the trees above his head. AUTHOR'S COLLECTION

his brother's life in Europe. He became a member of the 303rd Bomb Group Association. During my research, I got in contact with him and the plan was born for the Richters to travel to Holland. In early May 1997, Joe and his wife, Mildred, arrived on Schiphol airfield. The highlights of their stay in Holland were a visit to the place on the beach where Eldon's body was found and taking part in the annual May 4 remembrance ceremonies in Heemskerk. In his speech, the burgomaster of Heemskerk paid special attention to Eldon's sacrifice and the period that he rested in the Heemskerk soil. Flowers were laid, among others on Eldon's former gravesite, between two British war graves still in the cemetery. A day later, we visited the American Military Cemetery in Margraten and reflected, among others, near the final resting place of Bevan Colby and at the Walls of the Missing, on which the names of John Homan and Salvador Di Cosmo are inscribed.

May 4, 1997. Joe and Mildred Richter laying flowers on the grave in the Heemskerk Cemetery, where Joe's brother Eldon was buried from 1943 to 1946.

The final resting place of Tech Sgt. Eldon F. Richter of the 303rd Bomb Group in Waverly, Kansas. JOE E. RICHTER

With the passing of the years, the number of people who have firsthand knowledge of the events of World War II dwindles. I hope that this book may serve as a lasting tribute to all who lost their lives on August 19, 1943.

Appendix A: Losses and Casualties

U.S. ARMY AIR FORCE

96th Bomb Group

B-17F 42-30172 *Black Heart Jr*, 339th Bomb Squadron.
Crashed shortly after take-off due to mechanical troubles near Wolverton Sands, England. All crew safe.

P	2nd Lt.	Attaway, James A.
CP	2nd Lt.	Vinson, Matthew L.
N	2nd Lt.	Noderer, Charles O.
B	2nd Lt.	Miller, John R.
E	Tech Sgt.	Huff, Robert W.
RO	Tech Sgt.	Woods, Robert P.
BTG	Staff Sgt.	Moore, Lawrence L.
LWG	Staff Sgt.	Garrow, Richard D.
RWG	Staff Sgt.	Kangles, John A.
TG	Staff Sgt.	Trujillo, John E.
OB	Col.	Travis, James E.

303rd Bomb Group

B-17F 42-3192, 358th Bomb Squadron.
Shot down by fighters and crashed in Raamsdonksveer.

P	1st Lt.	Nix, James S.	KIA	Margraten, H-11-22*
CP	2nd Lt.	Shebeck, Daniel A.	KIA	Margraten, H-11-1
N	2nd Lt.	Curo, Dwight M.	POW	
B	1st Lt.	Solverson, Robert K.	KIA	USA, Wisconsin
E	Tech Sgt.	Krajacic, Frank G.	KIA	Margraten, K-7-11
RO	Tech Sgt.	Brooke, Curtis O.	POW	
BTG	Staff Sgt.	Perez, Frank F.	POW	
LWG	Staff Sgt.	Buck, George W.	POW	
RWG	Staff Sgt.	Gross, Joseph	POW	
TG	Staff Sgt.	Boyd, Fred W.	POW	
OB	1st Lt.	Moffatt, Louis T.	POW	

*Nix apparently received a posthumous promotion. His rank in the mission reports of the 303rd Bomb Group is first lieutenant, while his headstone in Margraten bears the rank of captain.

B-17F 42-5392 *Stric Nine*, 427th Bomb Squadron.
Shot down by fighters and crashed off Hook of Holland in the North Sea.

P	2nd Lt.	Quillen, Lauren H.	KIA	USA, Colorado
CP	2nd Lt.	Homan, John R.	MIA	Margraten, Walls of the Missing
N	2nd Lt.	Colby Jr, Bevan W.	KIA	Margraten, M-13-17
B	2nd Lt.	Irish, William N.	KIA	USA, Colorado
E	Tech Sgt.	Richter, Eldon F.	KIA	USA, Kansas
RO	Staff Sgt.	DiCosmo, Salvador J.	MIA	Margraten, Walls of the Missing
BTG	Staff Sgt.	Price, Elbert O.	POW	
LWG	Staff Sgt.	Brown, Joe H.	POW	
RWG	Staff Sgt.	Abernathy, Paul W.	POW	
TG	Staff Sgt.	Sauer, Arthur K.	POW	

305th Bomb Group

B-17F 42-29807 *Lady Liberty*, 364th Bomb Squadron.
Shot down by flak and crashed in Westerscheldt near Borssele.

P	1st Lt.	Miller, Ralph R.	POW	
CP	2nd Lt.	Meade, John F.	KIA	USA, Massachusetts
N	2nd Lt.	McGowan, Donald J.	KIA	USA, New Jersey
B	2nd Lt.	McGinley, Joseph M.	KIA	Neuville-en-Condroz, B-42-49
E	Tech Sgt.	Crabtree, Bynum G.	KIA	USA, North Carolina
RO	Tech Sgt.	Horn, Fulton F.	KIA	USA, Texas
BTG	Staff Sgt.	Miller Jr, Albert F.	MIA	Margraten, Walls of the Missing
LWG	Sgt.	Crough, William J.	KIA	Neuville-en-Condroz, D-12-52
RWG	Staff Sgt.	Lott, Edgar G.	MIA	Margraten, Walls of the Missing
TG	Staff Sgt.	Radosevich, Emil	POW	

381st Bomb Group

B-17F 42-3101, 533rd Bomb Squadron.
Shot down by fighters and crashed in Rozenburg.

P	1st Lt. Koenig, Orlando H.	POW
CP	2nd Lt. Mangarpan Jr, Joseph L.	POW
N	1st Lt. Spivey, Leonard L.	POW
B	2nd Lt. O'Loughlin, Edward T.	POW

E	Tech Sgt. Perkins, Leo I.	POW	
RO	Tech Sgt. Chester, Russell G.	POW	
BTG	Staff Sgt. Buran, Walter J.	KIA	Margraten, J-3-19
LWG	Staff Sgt. Everett, Arthur L.	KIA	Margraten, J-3-11
RWG	Staff Sgt. Jones, Wilbert G.	KIA	Margraten, H-17-17
TG	Staff Sgt. Sabourin, Eugene A.	KIA	USA, Massachusetts

388th Bomb Group

B-17F 42-30068, 561st Bomb Squadron.
Shot down by flak and fighters and crashed in Haamstede.

P	2nd Lt. Howe Jr, Benjamin.	KIA	USA, New York
CP	2nd Lt. Gruhn, Paul R.	KIA	USA, Wisconsin
N	2nd Lt. Pilley, Arthur G.	POW	
B	2nd Lt. Tutt, Joel H.	POW	
E	Staff Sgt. Connelly, George E.	KIA	USA, Pennsylvania
RO	Staff Sgt. Toth, Stephen A.	KIA	USA, New York
BTG	Staff Sgt. Butt, Dale T.	KIA	USA, Wisconsin
LWG	Staff Sgt. Hillier, James E.	KIA	USA, New York
RWG	Staff Sgt. Ryan, William G.	KIA	USA, New York
TG	Staff Sgt. Stamp, William J.	KIA	USA, New York

56th Fighter Group

P-47C 41-6216, 63rd Fighter Squadron.
Forced to ditch due to mechanical troubles in Haringvliet near Hellevoetsluis.

| P | 2nd Lt. Hodges, Glenn L. | POW | |

ROYAL AIR FORCE

131 Squadron

Spitfire VB AR371. Shot down by fighters and crashed in the Channel off Dungeness, England.

F/Sgt Parry, R.K.   safe, picked up by Air Sea Rescue

174 Squadron

Typhoon IB JP550. Crashed due to mechanical troubles in the Channel off Le Touquet, France.

P/O O'Callaghan, E.   safe, picked up by Air Sea Rescue

182 Squadron

Typhoon IB JP552. Shot down by fighters and crashed near Amiens, France.

F/Sgt Dench, R. L. H.   evaded back to UK

Typhoon IB R8927. Shot down by fighters and crashed near Amiens, France.
F/O Fraleigh, M. I.   KIA   Beauval, C-1-A

Typhoon IB EK395. Shot down by fighters and crashed near Amiens, France.
F/Lt Ball, G. F.   POW

316 (Polish) Squadron
Spitfire IX EN179. Shot down by fighters and crashed near Naours, France.
F/O Prochnicki, A. F.   KIA   Grainville-Langannerie, 2-AA-11

421 (Canadian) Squadron
Spitfire IX MA543. Shot down by fighters and crashed in the Somme estuary, France.
P/O Joyce, F.C.   POW

LUFTWAFFE

Jagdgeschwader 1
Me 109 G-6 20525 *Weisse 6*, 7./JG 1. Shot down by B-17 gunners and crashed in the North Sea, off Hook of Holland.
Uffz Gustav Schulze   safe

Me 109 G-6 ? *Weisse 5*, 7./JG 1. Shot down by B-17 gunners and belly landed near Oud Rozenburg. Pilot probably:
Lt Hermannes   safe

Me 109 G-6 15367 *Schwarze 1*, 8./JG 1. Shot down by Spitfire and crashed 1.5 kilometers northwest of Zuidzande, north-west of Oostburg.
Oblt Herwig Zuzic   KIA   Ysselsteyn, BB-9-202

Me 109 G-6 15472 *Schwarze 8*, 8./JG 1. Shot down by Spitfire and belly-landed near Cadzand-haven.
Unknown pilot   safe

Me 109 G-6 15612, 8./JG 1. Shot down by Spitfire and belly landed near Het Zoute.
Unknown pilot   safe

Me 109 G-6 20498 *Gelbe 3*, 9./JG 1. Shot down by Spitfire and crashed northeast of Philippine.
Lt Horst Bork   KIA   Ysselsteyn, BB-9-203

Me 109 G-6 19992 *Gelbe 12*, 9./JG 1. Shot down by Spitfire and belly-landed near Walsoorden (near Perkpolder ferry).
Fw Hans Meissner   WIA

Me 109 G-6 20092 *Gelbe 11*, 9./JG 1. Shot down by Spitfire and crashed east of Groede, northeast of Oostburg.
Lt Hans Joachim Niemeyer   MIA

Me 109 G-6 20521, III./JG 1. Shot down by B-17 gunners and crashed on De Beer Island, near Rozenburg.
Unknown pilot   WIA

Me 109 G-6 15464, III./JG 1. Made emergency-landing due to fuel shortage at an unknown location.
Unknown pilot   safe

Jagdgeschwader 2
Me 109 G-6 15288, 4./JG 2. Shot down by Spitfire and crashed near Abbeville-Drucat, France.
Uffz Heinz Köckler   KIA   Bourdon/Somme, 32-8-285

Me 109 G-6 19875 *Weisse 26*, 5./JG 2. Shot down by Spitfire in Epinoy/Pas-de-Calais area, France.
Lt Hans Joachim Rimarski   MIA

Me 109 G-6 15385, II./JG 2. Shot down by Spitfire and crashed near Neufchatel-en-Bray, France.
Uffz Gustav Sens   WIA

Jagdgeschwader 3
Me 109 ? *Gelbe 8*, 8./JG 3. Shot down by P-47 and crashed near Loon op Zand.
Unknown pilot   safe

Jagdgeschwader 26
FW 190 A-5 1091 *Weisse 4*, 1./JG 26. Shot down by P-47 and crashed near Eethen.
Lt Leberecht Altmann   safe

FW 190 ? *Schwarze 7*, 2./JG 26. Shot down by P-47 and belly-landed near Vinkenbroek, west of Roosendaal.
Uffz Jan Schild   safe

FW 190 A-5 2405 *Weisse 2*, 4./JG 26. Shot down by Spitfire 2,5 kilometers northeast of Amiens, France.
Uffz Martin Günther   WIA

FW 190 A-5 52654, 6./JG 26. Emergency landing on airfield Poix, France as a result of severe combat damage during afternoon mission.
Unknown pilot   safe

Me 109 G-4 19783 *Weisse 3*, 7./JG 26. Shot down by B-17 gunners and crashed near Waspik in Maas river.
Fw Wilhelm Mensing   WIA

Me 109 G-4 14996, 7./JG 26. Crashed due to unknown cause near Brecht, Belgium.
Unknown pilot   safe

Me 109 G-6 16394 *Gelbe 12*, 9./JG 26. Shot down by B-17 gunners and crashed in Waalwijk.
Uffz Werner Möszner   WIA

FW 190 A-5 2620, 10./JG 26. Shot down by Spitfires during afternoon mission and crashed near Villers-Bretonneux, 50 km southeast of Amiens, France.
Oblt Johannes Meyer   KIA   Bourdon/Somme, 32-9-336

Me 109 G-4 19373 *Schwarze 3*, 12./JG 26. Shot down by P-47 and crashed in the Breda area.
Lt Werner Grupe   WIA

Nachtjagdgeschwader 1
Me 110 G-4 6224, I./NJG 1. Destroyed on Gilze-Rijen airfield by American bombs.

Other German casualties
Killed by American bombs in East-/West-Souburg:
Obergefreiter Eric Berg   Missing
Oberfeldwebel Willi Kahle   Ysselsteyn, BB-8-199
Obergefreiter Frans Schütz   Ysselsteyn, BB-9-201
Oberjäger 2. Klasse Hermann Steinhof   Ysselsteyn, BB-8-200

Probably killed by American bombs in Gilze-Rijen:
Lt Gerhard Meijer   Ysselsteyn, AZ-8-76

DUTCH CIVILIANS

Souburg and surroundings:

Hendrik Barentsen	47 years
Willem F. Damen	29 years
Adriana J. Damen-Tabbernee	23 years
Willem F. Diermanse	28 years
Adriana Holthuyzen-de Wolff	68 years
Mattheus Lorier	49 years
Egidia P. J. Minderhoud-Vlijberge	35 years
Maria Olyslager-Dorleijn	67 years
Amalia Ch. Fr. Palmkoeck-van Wijnbergen	60 years
Hendrik W. van Rijk	42 years
Tannetje van Rijk-Louwerse	39 years
Adriana Chr. H. Suurmond-Theune	43 years
Sara C. Suurmond	4 months
Maria Wouters	11 years

Hulten and surroundings:

Henricus W.A. Aarts	20 years
Antoinetta M. Akkermans-van Gils	46 years
Johannes G. Akkermans	12 years
Maria H. Akkermans	6 years
Adrianus J. Anssems	37 years
Cornelia M. van Beek	17 years
Cornelis Broeders	54 years
Leonardus A. Broeders	23 years
Maria C. Broeders-Kennis	49 years
Cornelia van Dongen-van Riel	64 years
Petronella van Dongen-de Bont	57 years
Johannes W. Eestermans	23 years
Johanna W.A. Eestermans-de Jong	31 years
Cornelia A.M. Faes	10 years
Marinus C.J. de Graaf	25 years
Cornelis Graauwmans	1 year
Petrus J. Graauwmans	12 years
Thomas J. Graauwmans	10 years
Gerard Hoogenhuizen	18 years
Cornelia M. Michielsen	3 years
Franciscus P. Michielsen	2 years
Petrus F. Michielsen	5 months
Cornelis Quak	25 years

Appendix B: German Units, Ranks, and Abbreviations

The reader will come across three different sizes of German units in this book: the *Geschwader*, the *Gruppe* (plural: *Gruppen*), and the *Staffel* (plural: *Staffeln*). These terms have not been translated.

A *Geschwader* was made up of three *Gruppen* and a *Gruppe* of three *Staffeln*. The *Gruppe* was the all-important tactical unit. It was composed of approximately thirty fighters, all of the same type and usually based on the same airfield. It normally went into action as a complete unit under the tactical leadership of its commanding officer, the *Gruppenkommandeur*.

In this book, the standard abbreviations for German units are used. The day fighter *Jagdgeschwader* is shortened to JG. The night-fighter *Nachtjagdgeschwader* is NJG, and the bomber *Kampfgeschwader* is KG.

Roman numerals before the JG and ordinary numerals after it signify the *Gruppe* and the *Geschwader* number, respectively. For example, I./JG 26 was the First *Gruppe* of *Jagdgeschwader* 26.

Within the *Gruppen*, the *Staffeln* were usually evenly distributed. The first three belonged to the first *Gruppe*; the fourth, fifth, and sixth *Staffeln* to the second *Gruppe*; and so on.

The *Staffel* number also preceeded the JG and, if used, replaced the *Gruppe* number. For example, 1./JG 26 was the First *Staffel* of *Jagdgeschwader* 26; it automatically belonged to its First *Gruppe*.

German ranks are also not translated. A rough comparison to the American ranks is presented here. Many German pilots were non-commissioned officers; where necessary, the abbreviations are given.

Colonel	*Oberst*
Lieutenant Colonel	*Oberstleutnant*
Major	*Major*
Captain	*Hauptmann*
First Lieutenant	*Oberleutnant* (Oblt)
Second Lieutenant	*Leutnant* (Lt)
Flight Officer	*Stabsfeldwebel*
Master Sergeant	*Oberfeldwebel/Hauptfeldwebel*
Staff Sergeant	*Feldwebel/Unterfeldwebel* (Fw/Ufw)
Sergeant	*Unteroffizier* (Uffz)

215

Acknowledgments

In the first place, I am very much indebted to my dear friends Dick and Marjorie Johnson. They hosted me during my research period in the National Archives in Washington, D.C., and like two previous times, they made me feel very welcome and at home in beautiful downtown Deale.

Special thanks also go to John W. Archer from Bungay, England, for proofreading my manuscript and correcting my grammar. All errors that are left are mine alone.

I am very honored and grateful that Col. Kermit D. Stevens, former commanding officer of the 303rd Bomb Group, was willing to write the foreword for this book.

I was privileged to have the full cooperation of many veterans and historians during my research. Thanks to their stories, I was able to use the style of writing I had in mind when I started my research: a framework of official reports brought to life by the stories and pictures of the men who made it all happen. In the United States, help was provided by the following veterans, their relatives, or historians: Paul W. Abernathy, Howard L. Abney, James A. Attaway, George P. Birdsong, Curtis O. Brooke, Joe H. Brown, Donald L. Caldwell, Russell G. Chester, Harold E. Comstock, Robert E. Doherty, Richard C. Fortunak, Frank Frison, Carl J. Fyler, Don Gamble, William A. Gottschalk, the late Joseph Gross, Darrell D. Gust, Charles E. Harris, Anita H. Hodges, the late Edward J. Huntzinger, Vernon L. Iverson, Asay B. Johnson, Kristine Koenig, Lois M. Koenig, Paul C. Lemann, Everett F. Malone, Joseph L. Mangarpan, Robert L. Mattison, Mary Martha McIntyre, William D. McSween Jr., Debbie Miller Hughes, Roger V. Miller, Louis T. Moffatt, Curtis Olsen, Brian D. O'Neill, Frank F. Perez, George R. Redhead, Arthur J. Robinson, Arthur K. Sauer, the late William E. Shields, F. Robert Spitznagel, Leonard L. Spivey, Alexander C. Strickland, Charles R. Terry, John H. Truluck Jr., Joel H. Tutt, Matthew L. Vinson, George W. Vogel, and Leroy C. Wilcox.

I would especially like to mention the help of Hazel Bengtson, Larry Hutchings, Joe and Mildred Richter, and Thomas G. Toth, who lost family members on August 19, 1943.

The assistance provided by Harry D. Gobrecht was outstanding. He, the author of the 303rd Bomb Group's history *Might in Flight*, tirelessly provided me with many details about this group, its crews, and its planes.

Several veterans, good friends, and historians in England also assisted me. They are Doug Castle, Roy A. Crane, Ronald L.H. Dench, William Donald, Roger A. Freeman, Bill Ireson, Ron MacKay, Martin Middlebrook, David R. Osborne, and Geoffrey Ward.

A very special contributor to this book was German veteran pilot Werner Möszner. He and his wife visited the site of his near-fatal crash-landing on August 19, 1943, with me.

Others who provided help were Michael M. LeBlanc in Canada; Werner Christie, and Kristian Nyerrod in Norway; Janusz Zuziak in Poland; and Tony Gaze in Australia.

Many members of the Dutch Airwar Study Group 1939–1945 were of great help. They are Dick Breedijk, Hendrik Cazemier, Hans de Haan, Jan A. Hey, Ab A. Jansen, Harold E. Jansen, A.P. de Jong, Erwin van Loo, Rob van den Nieuwendijk, P. Pouwels, John Prooi, M. Sanderse, the late Hans van Soest, J. Tuynman, Rob W. de Visser, and Jacques de Vos. Wout J. van den Hout was a fantastic help for the Gilze-Rijen part of the book. Again, this Airwar Study Group has proven itself to be a true source of information and support.

Another special word of thanks is for Father Gerard Thuring. As a boy, he was an eyewitness of the demise of one of the B-17s on August 19, 1943. Now, as chairman of the historical section of the Liberation Museum in Groesbeek, he was instrumental in getting this story published. Thanks also to the other members of the historical section, especially Marco Cillessen and Gerrie Franken, for valuable comments on the manuscript.

Others in Holland who provided help were Mr. Jac Biemans (Waalwijk), C. Coenders (General Maczek Museum), Mrs. S. Diermanse, Mr. Louis Kaulartz (Army Historical Branch), Mrs. W. L. Looise (Flushing), Mr. A. Meerman (Flushing), Mr. H. J. A. Stuurman (Rozenburg), Mrs. J. Steenhuis (Dutch railway company), Mr. Hans Sakkers, Mr. G. C. J. Uyt de Haag, Mr. Andries Westendorp, Mr. Beerend Wietsma, and Mr. R. J. E. M. van Zinnicq Bergmann.

The following official institutions provided material or information: Bundesarchiv/Militärarchiv (Freiburg i.B), Deutsche Dienststelle (Berlin), Public Record Office (London), the Polish Institute and Sikorsky Museum (London), Forsvarsmuseet (Oslo), Riksarkivet (Oslo), National Archives (Washington, D.C.), and the National Air and Space Museum (Washington, D.C.).

Last, but certainly not least, I owe many thanks to my wife, Hester. She not only patiently endured the countless hours I spent researching the August 19, 1943, mission hidden in my study, but also urged me to go to Washington for additional research in the National Archives, hosted American, German, British, and Dutch veterans and friends in our home, and always encouraged me to continue.

Many, many thanks to you all.

Index

Stackpole Military History Series

MISSION 376
BATTLE OVER THE REICH, MAY 28, 1944
Ivo de Jong

Some of the U.S. Eighth Air Force's bombing missions of World War II, such as the raid on the ball-bearing factories at Schweinfurt, became legendary. Many others did not, but these more routine missions formed an important part of Allied strategy. One of them was Mission 376 on May 28, 1944, when more than 1,200 American B-17s and B-24s took off from bases in England and headed for targets inside Germany, where Luftwaffe fighters scrambled to beat them back. With unprecedented and enthralling detail, this book describes an "ordinary" bombing mission during World War II.

Paperback • 6 x 9 • 448 pages • 329 b/w photos

WWW.STACKPOLEBOOKS.COM
1-800-732-3669

Stackpole Military History Series

THE SAVAGE SKY
LIFE AND DEATH ON A BOMBER OVER GERMANY IN 1944

George Webster

The life expectancy of an American B-17 crew in Europe during World War II was eleven missions, yet crews had to fly twenty-five—and eventually thirty—before they could return home. Against these long odds the bomber crews of the U.S. 8th Air Force, based in England, joined the armada of Allied aircraft that pummeled Germany day after day. Radioman George Webster recounts the terrors they confronted: physical and mental exhaustion, bitter cold at high altitudes, lethal shrapnel from flak, and German fighters darting among bombers like feeding sharks.

Paperback • 6 x 9 • 256 pages • 21 photos

WWW.STACKPOLEBOOKS.COM
1-800-732-3669

Stackpole Military History Series

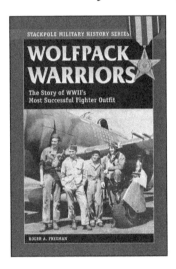

WOLFPACK WARRIORS
THE STORY OF WWII'S
MOST SUCCESSFUL FIGHTER OUTFIT
Roger A. Freeman

"Beware the Thunderbolt!" With that motto, the pilots of the
U.S. 56th Fighter Group took to the skies above Europe in
their P-47 Thunderbolt fighters as part of the Eight Air Force's
war against the Third Reich. The men of the 56th—also known
as Zemke's Wolfpack—escorted bombers into Germany,
tangled with the Luftwaffe, and carried out gound-attack
missions in support of the Allied invasion. They pioneered
fighter tactics and compiled a staggering record: 665.5 aerial
kills, 311 ground kills, 39 aces, 2 Distinguished Unit Citations,
18 Distinguished Service Crosses, and 29 Silver Stars.

Paperback • 6 x 9 • 288 pages • 85 b/w photos

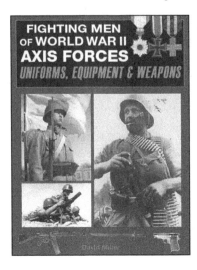
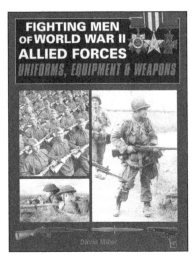